Protecting Your Garden From Animal Damage

Created and designed by
the editorial staff of
ORTHO BOOKS

Project Editor
Marianne Lipanovich

Writer
Gregory A. Giusti

Designer
Gary Hespenheide

Ortho Books

Publisher
Robert B. Loperena

Editorial Director
Christine Jordan

Manufacturing Manager
Ernie S. Tasaki

Editors
Robert J. Beckstrom
Michael D. Smith

Managing Editor
Sally W. Smith

Prepress Supervisor
Linda M. Bouchard

Editorial Assistants
Joni Christiansen
Sally J. French

Acknowledgments

Technical Consultant
Robert M. Corrigan, Ph.D.

Illustrator
Pamela Manley

Photography Editor
Susan Friedman

Editorial Coordinator
Cass Dempsey

Copyeditor
David Sweet

Manuscript Editor
Cheryl Smith

Proofreader
Fran Taylor

Indexer
Trisha Feuerstein

Special Thanks to
Deborah Cowder

Separations by
Color Tech Corp.

Lithographed in the USA by
Webcrafters, Inc.

Photographers
Names of photographers are followed by the page numbers on which their work appears.
R = right, C = center, L = left, T = top, B = bottom.

Laurie Black/Ortho Information Services: 4–5
Jerry Clark: 12–13, 15T, 50, 53B, 67, 69, 73, 85T, 85B
Josephine Coatsworth/Ortho Information Services: 8
John Coleman: 22
Scott Craven: 7, 35B, 45, 46, 49R, 71, 72, 88, 89T
W. Paul Gorenzel: 25, 58, 64, 65, 68
Susan Friedman: 31, 89B
Pat Kaiser: 35T
Michael Landis/Ortho Information Services: 87B
Tom & Pat Leeson: 40
Rex Marsh: 17B
Michael McKinley/Ortho Information Services: 9
R. O'Connell: 70, 84B
Ortho Information Services: 11, 49L, 63, 66, 87T
Barry L. Runk/Grant Heilman: front cover TL
Superstock: front cover TR, front cover BL, front cover BR, 1, 6, 10, 14, 15B, 21, 23, 32–33, 34, 38, 39, 44, 47, 54–55, 56, 57T, 74, 75, 76, 77, 78–79, 80, 81, 82, 83, 86, 90, 92

Front Cover
Top left: Starlings are pests over most of the country.
Top right: Raccoons are becoming troublesome even in some urban areas.
Bottom left: An underground dweller, a mole eats insects and earthworms.
Bottom right: Because of their size and intelligence, deer can be the most damaging garden visitors.

Title Page
Even the cutest creature can damage your garden.

Back Cover
The reward for a pest-free garden is beauty and abundance.

Address all inquiries to:
Ortho Books
Box 5006
San Ramon, CA 94583-0906

1	2	3	4	5	6	7	8	9
94	95	96	97	98	99			

ISBN 0-89721-267-3
Library of Congress Catalog Card
Number 94-65699

THE SOLARIS GROUP
2527 Camino Ramon
San Ramon, CA 94583

Protecting Your Garden From Animal Damage

Principles of Animal Pest Management

Learning to control the damage caused by wildlife will let you still enjoy their company in the garden.

Once you have established that an animal is causing damage in your garden, you need to determine the species responsible. Check your garden for obvious signs of damage, such as gnawing, bark girdling, chewing, and even the complete removal of the surface of a plant. If a plant is wilting or drooping, check the root area or the portion of the main stem below the ground. In many cases, you will find that the roots have been chewed or totally consumed. These signs will give you clues as to which animal or animals may be causing the damage.

Often the removal of pests, usually by lethal methods, is put forward as the only effective solution to animal pest problems. This book offers lethal removal solutions when appropriate, but within the overall goal of damage management.

Before deciding to kill an animal pest, you first should explore methods of nonlethal removal or exclusion. There are a number of options to choose from. To make the best choice, it is important to learn what species is the guilty party, the habits of that species, and the strategies available to remove the species.

In general, vertebrate species are creatures of habit. Taking the time to recognize and understand their habits will enable you to better regulate unwanted behavior.

A garden need not be heavily fortified to protect it from some of the more common animal pests.

BASIC REQUIREMENTS FOR VERTEBRATE SPECIES

All species of animals have similar biological requirements for food, water, shelter, and space. The need for food and water is easily understood; animals require the same nourishment as humans do.

Shelter protects animals from predators and the elements. Shelter also provides animals with a safe place to raise their young and proximity to food and water. The need for shelter is shared by all vertebrates, including humans.

The need for space, the fourth biological requirement, varies among the vertebrate species. Like people, most species of animals find overcrowded conditions uncomfortable.

Unlike people, however, some species are so protective of their space that they will vigorously defend it against rivals, intruders, and predators. One animal pest, the pocket gopher, is an excellent example of a highly territorial species. Although a pocket gopher's territory is smaller than that of a grizzly bear or deer, it will feverishly defend this space if the other necessities of life—food, water, and shelter—are being threatened.

HABITATS AND HABITS

The area that provides an animal with all of its basic survival needs—food, water, shelter, and space—is known as habitat. The geographic area that includes all these physical require-

A garden harvest that you are proud of is equally appealing to wildlife. Although you may never eliminate all animal pests, you can control the damage they do to your garden.

ments makes up the individual animal's home range, or territory.

The home ranges of species vary greatly in size. The home range of a pocket gopher may be only 100 square feet while that of a deer may be one square mile. It is important to know the approximate size of an animal pest's home range. If, for example, an animal is traveling considerable distances to and from your garden, your choice of damage management options is limited.

If habitat refers to where an animal lives, then habit refers to the behavior of an individual animal or species. For example, as they approach the surface of the soil when excavating a burrow system, moles construct mounds that are cone shaped while pocket gophers construct mounds that are crescent shaped. Knowing about telltale signs like mound shape is important when trying to determine the species causing the damage.

Finally, it is also important to be aware of species distribution. Some animal pests live only in certain areas of the country. If, for example, shrew moles do not occur in your section of the country, you can strike them from your list of pest candidates.

MANAGEMENT OPTIONS

Options for animal pest management fall into two categories: lethal and nonlethal. Lethal methods result in the death of the animal pest while nonlethal methods spare the animal's life.

Lethal Methods

Lethal methods include toxic baits, trapping, and shooting. Because these methods cause the target animal to die, before using them you should take extra care to identify the damage and the individual or species and to choose a method that won't harm other animals. Also, if a species other than a common garden pest is causing damage, such as a skunk, there may be federal, state, or local regulations for removing it. Before using any lethal method, contact your cooperative extension office or resource management agency to determine whether the species is covered by special regulations.

Baiting Toxic baits were once based on pure grains such as wheat, bran, and oats, preferred foods of common animal pests. Modern baits are often a mixture of grains formed into pel-

lets. Because these baits have proved less attractive to animal pests than those based solely on pure grains, they must be presented in their freshest form if they are to be readily accepted by the target animal. Baits that are old, moldy, wet, or in any other state of decay are undesirable and may be ignored by the animal.

Before purchasing toxic baits, take time to read the instructions on the label. Toxic baits often carry restrictions on use, placement, and intended species.

Be aware that toxic baits can cause accidental or secondary poisoning. Accidental poisoning results when small children, family pets, and other nontarget animals consume toxic bait and either become ill or die. Secondary poisoning results when a predator eats a pest that has been poisoned, thereby ingesting the poison itself, and either becomes ill or dies.

Trapping Particularly for moles, pocket gophers, mice, and rats, trapping may be the best alternative if you have chosen a lethal method. Trapping confirms the identity of the damage-causing animal and helps pinpoint the source of future problems. There is no danger of accidental or secondary poisoning, although nontarget species can sometimes be caught in traps. Trapping is more an art than a science.

Methods of animal pest control vary widely; local nurseries or agricultural supply stores are able to advise you on the best controls for your needs.

Top: Exclusion is often the best nonlethal method of preventing animal damage to plants. Here, a completely enclosed garden keeps out birds and non-burrowing animals. Bottom: Sometimes the only protection that is necessary is raising the garden beds so that animals cannot enter them.

The key to effective trapping is practice, practice, practice.

Shooting   Though shooting an animal pest that has ruined a garden may bring emotional release, it is generally a poor choice. In many residential areas shooting is illegal as well as dangerous. Even in rural areas, the amount of time and energy involved in waiting for the animal pest to appear usually makes shooting impractical.

Nonlethal Methods

The list of nonlethal methods includes some that are extremely effective and others that could be categorized as modern-day snake oil. The main options are exclusion, repellents, frightening devices, live trapping, and aversives. In some cases, employing more than one method simultaneously is the best solution.

Exclusion   One of the most effective and long-lasting nonlethal strategies is exclusion—putting up fencing, screening, netting, or any other material that acts as a physical barrier between the animal pest and its intended destination. The goal is not only to deny the offending animal access to the area, but to change its behavior and redirect its efforts.

In recent years, technology has produced a number of new materials for exclusion protection. High-tensile material for permanent

Fencing Out Problems

Fences are a good exclusion method for minimizing damage caused by other large species such as dogs, cats, raccoons, opossums, and deer. When designing a fence to exclude animals you should try to incorporate all the necessary features (height, materials, mesh size) that will keep out any unwanted intruders.

A number of inexpensive electric fence charging units are on the market. Many are solar powered and require little maintenance. Others require household current or a conventional 12-volt automobile battery. When purchasing a charger you should consider the terrain where the fence will be placed, the surrounding areas, and the possibility of human interference. Most chargers have the potential of charging the fence with 500 volts, which is sufficient to repel even deer.

An effective electric fence for a garden is a single strand of electrified or "hot" wire placed 2½ to 3 feet off the ground, at a distance of 3 or 4 feet away from the plants—approximately chest high on a mature deer. As the deer walks up to the plants it will bump the wire and receive a shock. Minimal danger is posed to fawns and other animals that may otherwise become entangled in a more conventional woven wire fence.

Behavior modification is very important in minimizing deer damage. A simple way to train deer that the electric fence is "hot" is to attach strips of aluminum foil every 10 feet to the wire (make sure the fence is turned off!).

Then, spread peanut butter on the foil strips. After you have finished turn on the fence. When the deer approaches to investigate the peanut butter, it will receive a shock on the tip of its tongue or nose. This strong behavioral stimulus quickly teaches the deer to respect and avoid the fence.

Because all electric fencing is meant to carry high voltage but very low amperage, it gives a stinging shock but doesn't harm the animal. The idea behind electric fencing is to teach the animal to avoid it. Once an animal has received one or two strong shocks, it will usually leave the fence alone, even if the power is turned off. Touch the fence yourself if you want a demonstration of its efficiency.

Electric fencing is sensitive to conditions that cause the fence to "ground" itself and eliminate the sting. It is therefore important to minimize contact between the fence and the soil surface at all times. Be particular about weed control. Do not allow vegetation to come into contact with the wires. Additionally, if a fence is constructed beneath any trees or large shrubs, you must eliminate any contact between the fence and these plants. Grounding diverts much of the electrical current into the soil and reduces the effectiveness of the fence. Remember to attach warnings to your electric fences.

Finally, always remember to keep gates closed. Animal pests, like most other creatures, often choose the path of least resistance and readily enter a garden through an open gate.

Predators such as this red-shouldered hawk often prey on common animal pests.

Netting draped over berry bushes will keep birds away from the fruit.

fences and portable electric fences has broadened the scope of application to protect crops and gardens from large species such as deer and raccoons. Some gardeners have had success using materials underground, primarily wire mesh and wire baskets, for fossorial species such as moles, pocket gophers, and ground squirrels. For many pests, particularly birds, exclusion is the only legal option.

Repellents   By their taste, smell, or visibility, repellents discourage animals from damaging a plant. Because repellents are short lived, especially in wet weather, and can be easily washed from leaves by precipitation and irrigation, they have limited value in the garden. They often require multiple applications to be effective, and can sometimes adversely affect the plants they are designed to protect. In addition, individual animals may not be affected by them. Repellents generally work better when used with another nonlethal method.

Frightening devices   Although a wide variety of frightening devices, some quite expensive, are sold in nurseries and garden supply stores and through catalogs, this method has limited application. Animals can become accustomed to loud sounds, flashing lights, fake snakes, and nearly any other variation devised by manufacturers or gardeners. Rotating the frightening stimuli to different parts of the garden may increase effectiveness, but this practice alone rarely succeeds.

Live trapping   Live traps are more expensive than kill traps, but they have become more readily available to home gardeners. Live trapping requires some practice, but can bring gratifying results. When using live trapping, you must release the animal in a location where it will not become a problem for someone else. In suburban areas finding such a location may be difficult. Keep in mind that handling wild animals can be a formidable challenge.

Aversives   Aversives have very limited application in the garden and are currently being tested in more intensive agricultural settings. The target animal ingests the aversive, which makes the animal ill. Theoretically, the animal pest will then associate sickness with the plant or animal it ate and avoid the plant or animal in the future.

Below-Ground Pests

Some of the most common animal pests are never seen above the soil level.

Most gardeners have already been introduced to moles and pocket gophers, garden pests of the deep. These underground dwellers have in common with your garden a dependence on soil. Just as your plants derive nourishment from the soil, moles and pocket gophers obtain sustenance from the plants or insects that occur in the soil.

Although moles and pocket gophers may live close to each other in your garden (depending on where you live), the ways in which they cause damage differ. For example, moles are primarily insectivores, or insect eaters; pocket gophers are rodents, eating plants and seeds. Moles damage plants as they burrow in search of insects; gophers will eat the plants.

Moles and pocket gophers do not hibernate, so they must maintain their basal metabolic rate the year around. To do this they must eat throughout the winter months to provide themselves with the nourishment necessary for survival. In locations where snow covers the ground, you will not see signs of these animals, though they continue to do damage beneath the snow.

Underground dwellers, such as this pocket gopher, can inflict considerable damage on a garden without ever being seen above the ground.

MOLES

All moles in the United States and Canada belong to the family *Talpidae*. There are seven recognized species widely distributed throughout North America. Because of their subterranean habits, they are one of the least studied groups of native fauna. Most studies have focused on their physiological traits because laboratory studies, which tend to concentrate on physiology, are more convenient than field studies, which would concentrate on habits.

Generally, moles live in moist environments throughout the United States. They are usually absent from the arid lands of the Rocky Mountains, the Southwest, the Northwest, and most of Canada. Each of the seven species has a specific geographic range, and most gardeners who live in these ranges will eventually come across one of these species.

The coast mole (Scapanus orarius), *one of the Western species of moles, ranges from southeast British Columbia through Washington and Oregon to northwestern California.*

The Seven Species of North American Moles

The eastern mole (*Scalopus aquaticus*) is found in Texas, the Southeast, much of the Great Lakes region, and New England. It prefers moist sandy loam in lawns, gardens, and meadows. It usually avoids areas of dry soil.

Both the star-nosed mole (*Condylura cristata*) and the hairytail mole (*Parascalops breweri*) live in much of the northeastern United States and southeastern Canada. The star-nosed mole prefers low wet ground, often near streams or lakes. The hairytail mole is most often found in sandy loam soils where vegetation occurs.

Western species include the coast mole (*Scapanus orarius*), the broad-footed mole (*S. latimanus*), the Townsend's mole (*S. townsendii*), and the shrew or Gibb's mole (*Neu-*

rotrichus gibbsii). The Townsend's mole is found in southeast British Columbia, western Washington, and western Oregon. The coast mole shares this distribution but is also found in eastern Washington and eastern Oregon. Both species occur only in very local areas of northwestern California. The broad-footed mole is found primarily in the mountainous regions of California but is absent throughout the Central Valley. The shrew mole is found in the coastal regions of the Pacific Northwest.

The two most common species in the United States are the eastern mole and the Townsend's mole.

Description, Habit, and Habitat

All moles possess external physical features suited for an underground existence: streamlined body looking much like a large cigar; virtually no visible ears; eyes that could be described as pinholes; and limbs that are held out to the side, allowing moles to dig with a lateral-stroke motion that resembles a breast stroke. They vary in size from less than half an ounce (shrew mole) to nearly half a pound (Townsend's mole).

One of the most striking features of moles is their velvetlike fur. Its softness rivals that of any other fur-bearing mammal and was once prized for making fashionable coats. The fur has the unusual double lay; that is, each hair

*Top: The broad-footed mole (*Scapanus latimanus*) invades gardens in the mountainous regions of California. Bottom: The eastern mole (*Scalopus aquaticus*) can be found from New England to Texas.*

Mole Tunnel System

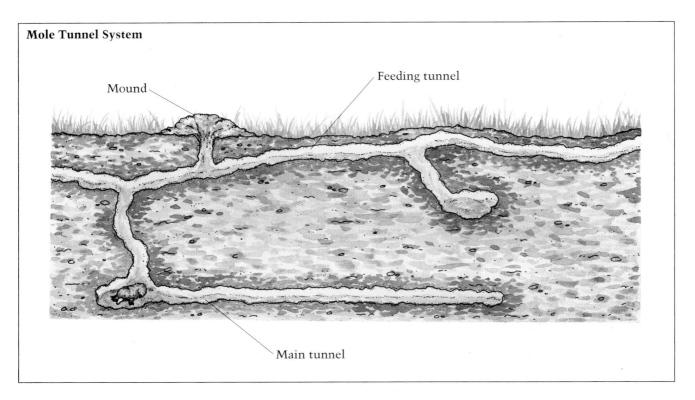

Mound

Feeding tunnel

Main tunnel

can rotate in the hair follicle and lay in either a forward or a backward position. This important feature allows the mole to back up in a narrow tunnel without its fur resisting.

All moles need to eat often. Because of their high metabolic rates, short digestive systems, and busyness, moles must consume relatively large percentages of their body weight daily to stay alive. This means that the animal must spend all its waking hours in search of food.

Moles construct two types of tunnel systems. The first, the surface runway so familiar to gardeners, is actually a feeding tunnel that moles dig in search of earthworms, grubs, and other food. Sometimes moles use a surface runway only once.

The other type of tunnel system, the burrow or main tunnel system, is much deeper and more permanent in design, serving as the living quarters for the animal. The Townsend's mole, for example, digs the main tunnel system to a depth of 9 feet, but most other species of moles dig to a depth of 12 to 18 inches.

Moles breed once a year, sometimes during late winter or early spring depending on geographic location. Though the exact length of the gestation period for North American moles is not known, it is generally assumed to be four to six weeks. Eastern moles are born from March to May and do not breed until they are a

year old. The coast, broad-footed, and Townsend's moles are born in March and April. The average litter size for all seven species is believed to be from two to five young. Moles are solitary animals, coming together only during the breeding season, although a family of two to five moles may sometimes inhabit an area for several months.

Damage Characteristics

It is essential for a gardener to learn to recognize the damage created by moles. In many areas they share their home range with pocket gophers or meadow mice, and management options differ for these animals.

Moles usually cause damage by their insatiable search for food or by their construction of deep tunnels. Their constant digging exposes plant roots, causing dessication, pushes bulbs from the ground, and damages turf and ground covers. In most cases plants are in the way as the moles search for earthworms, grubs, and other insects. Some plants the mole may accidentally ingest.

The soil disturbance created by their digging often encourages weed germination. This can add to the amount of time, energy, and herbicides needed to control weeds. The mounds are eyesores in turf and other ground covers, and can damage machinery such as lawn mowers.

Top: If it appears that a miniature volcano has suddenly erupted in your yard, there's a good chance you have a mole. Because moles plug their mounds from beneath the surface, the plug is nearly invisible when you view it from above. Bottom: Setting a scissor-jaw trap requires some skill, and moles are extremely wary of any new object in their tunnel systems.

Molehills or mounds are easily recognized. Moles push soil upward from beneath the tunnel entrance to the surface, leaving a mound that resembles a miniature volcano. These mounds can become quite large, looking like a load of soil dumped from a wheelbarrow. If you stood over a mound and looked directly down, you would have difficulty seeing the burrow opening because moles plug the hole from beneath the surface, rendering the opening nearly invisible. The absence of a visible plug is what distinguishes a molehill from a pocket gopher mound.

Management and Prevention Strategies

Moles are probably the most difficult garden pest to manage. They tend to be shy of traps, reluctant to ingest toxic grain baits, and secretive in their habits. It is therefore important to try various methods, separately and in combination.

Once you have detected molehills and surface runways in your yard, initiate the appropriate controls as soon as possible. It is much easier to stop one mole now than it is to stop ten moles at a later date.

Trapping Although limited in its effectiveness, trapping is still a recognized mole management tool. Setting traps in early spring can

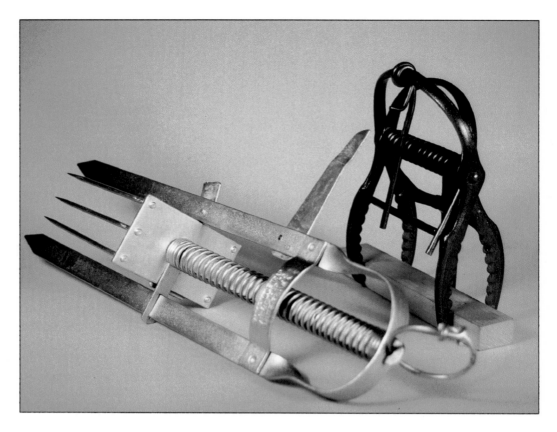

Check with local nursery personnel or your extension office to determine which mole traps will work best in your situation.

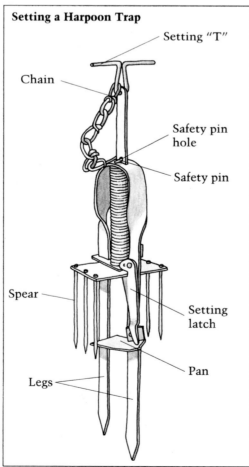

Setting a Harpoon Trap

Setting "T"

Chain

Safety pin hole

Safety pin

Spear

Setting latch

Pan

Legs

save you from having to contend with a whole family of moles in fall or next year. Because moles are active all year, you can set traps at any time. Be aware, however, that moles use their extremely sensitive noses and forepaws as tactile sensors to help guide them through their dark world. If they discover any new or strange object in their tunnel system, they will plug off that portion of the burrow and dig around or under the object. Laboratory tests on moles have demonstrated this fear of new objects, called neophobia, and you are wise to consider it when setting traps.

There are several types of mole traps available at nurseries, hardware stores, and garden supply stores. The most common are the harpoon, the scissor-jaw, and the noose, all of which are lethal. These traps, which are placed unbaited in an active surface runway or tunnel, all offer about the same rate of success, although the degree of skill required to set them successfully varies.

Because mole traps are expensive, most gardeners buy only one. Although one trap may solve your problem, increasing the number of traps improves your chances of success.

Before you set a mole trap you must first determine which tunnels or portions of the tunnels the moles are actively using. Remember, moles may use a surface runway only once and then abandon it. To locate active surface runways, step on a few sections and flatten them. Then, observe the sections daily for renewed signs of burrowing activity.

Once you have determined the areas of greatest activity, choose the most active portion of the surface runway or an area of the main tunnel system that is about 8 to 12 inches away from the mound or molehill. The deeper main tunnels are generally used for trapping the western species, while surface runways are more commonly used for eastern species.

To locate the underground tunnel leading up to the molehill, use a metal rod or wooden dowel to probe beneath the surface of the soil in a circular fashion, 8 to 12 inches from the molehill. You have located the tunnel when the probe slips through the surface of the tunnel and drops suddenly about 2 inches. The main tunnel is usually between two molehills.

A harpoon trap is set so that it sits above the tunnel. Begin by flattening a section of the tunnel. Next, center the trap over this section so the legs of the trap straddle the tunnel but will not penetrate it. Push the trap into the ground until the pan sits slightly above the flattened section. Form guide holes in the ground with the spears by setting the latch in the raised position. Holding the trap firmly to prevent the legs from moving, pull on the setting "T" to raise and lower the spears into the ground.

Once you have formed the guide holes, drop the setting latch into the operating position, taking care that the end of the latch falls outside of the pan lip. Hold the trap firmly in place and pull the setting "T" up until the trap locks in the set position. Insert the safety pin through the hole in the handle. Make sure the trap pan is resting just above the tunnel so that only the tips of the spears are in the ground and the spears don't block the tunnel. When the trap is positioned, remove the safety pin (see the illustration opposite).

The scissor-jaw trap is set in the main runway. With a shovel or hand trowel, dig out just enough of the main tunnel so that the trap will fit into it. Build a plug of soil in the center of the opened tunnel. Lower the trap (with the safety latch in place) into the open tunnel so that the trigger pan is sitting squarely on the soil plug. Be careful that no part of the trap

other than the trigger pan protrudes into the mole's tunnel. Next, sift loose dirt over the trap to about the level of the coil spring. Finally, release the safety latch.

To set a noose trap, dig across the tunnel to expose an area just slightly deeper than the tunnel and the width of the trap. Place the trap in the tunnel so the jaws or the loop straddle or enclose the runway. Block the tunnel with loose soil, packing the soil firmly beneath the trigger pan so that the trigger rests snugly on the built-up section. Then, fill the hole with dirt to cover the trap to the level of the trigger pan.

Simply setting the trap in an active runway or tunnel does not guarantee a captured mole. Patience and persistence are key. Occasionally the mole discovers the trap and buries it with soil. If this happens, clean out the tunnel and try again. The animal will probably revisit the site within 24 hours.

All traps should be checked daily to ensure they are in working order. If you haven't caught the mole within three days, move the trap to another location. Remember, moles are solitary animals. Except during the breeding season and the few months following the birth of a litter, usually only one mole inhabits a tunnel system.

If you are lucky enough to catch a mole, flatten the other mounds, surface runways, and tunnels. If they rise up again, then you have more than one mole. Repeat the process of identifying the most active tunnel or runway and choosing where to set the trap. Bury the dead mole in the tunnel system or contact local wildlife resource agencies for other legal disposal methods.

Baiting Although baiting is a common practice, it is not always effective. Because moles need to sustain a high basal metabolic rate, they must eat food high in protein. To do this, moles feed on animal prey. Unfortunately, all the available commercial baits are made from cereal grains. These baits don't provide enough protein and are therefore unappealing to moles.

However, baits are more economical and easier to use than traps. If you are being plagued by moles over a large area you may want to consider toxic baits as part of an overall management strategy that includes other methods. It is unlikely that toxic baits alone will produce satisfactory results. Before using toxic baits, always read and follow the label directions.

Stalking Some gardeners can detect mole movements by observing the ridges caused by the mole's feeding just under the surface. Many believe this activity is most evident in early morning or early evening. If you have a watchful eye, patience, and initiative, stand ready with a shovel. When the mole gives away its location, capture it alive by scooping it out with a shovel. Place the mole in a bucket or other container and release it in an area away from people. You can use a pitchfork, instead of a shovel, to impale and kill the mole. Always wear protective clothing and gloves. Bury the mole in the tunnel system or contact local wildlife resource agencies for other legal disposal methods.

Fumigants Commercially manufactured smoke bombs are available from your local nursery, hardware store, or garden supply store. Made of a sulfur compound, they are ignited and placed into the main tunnel system. The resulting smoke penetrates the tunnel and suffocates the animal if it is close to the smoke bomb. However, if the mole is in a secluded portion of the tunnel or in a side tunnel, it will smell the pungent sulfur long before the smoke reaches toxic levels. Once the mole has detected the smell, it will instinctively plug that portion of the tunnel to keep the smoke from lethally penetrating the system.

Using smoke bombs presents serious safety problems. Because they are ignited, a gardener who is careless or unskillful can suffer severe burns or let loose an uncontrollable fire. Smoke bombs are generally not very successful against moles, and should not be considered a serious management approach. If you do use them, study label directions and follow them carefully and exactly.

Some gardeners devise their own fumigation systems, directing the exhaust from their lawn mower or other gas-powered equipment with a hose into the tunnel system (see below). Carbon monoxide is deadly and has the advantage of being odorless, but such a system may not force the gas to penetrate the tunnel system completely. Never use engine exhaust near houses or other buildings. Escaping gases can kill people and pets if concentrations accumulate in enclosed areas.

Flooding Some gardeners have had limited success flooding the tunnels and runways with a garden hose. This method can be effective if the area is relatively free of bushes or dense ground cover that could hide the mole once it escapes. After the mole is forced out of the tunnels and into the open, the gardener must be quick to dispatch the animal with a shovel or hoe, or catch it on a shovel, place it in a bucket, and release the animal in an area away from people.

You can devise your own fumigation system using gas-powered equipment, but only use such a system away from people, pets, and buildings.

Exclusion   It may be possible to exclude moles from a small garden. To do so, build a fence of wire mesh that extends at least 6 inches above the ground and 18 inches below the ground. At the bottom, bend the fencing material outward, away from the garden, to discourage digging.

Habitat alterations   Because moles need to maintain their basal metabolic rate the year around, they are constantly in search of food. A comprehensive soil insect control program involving insecticides may ultimately reduce overall mole populations by removing their food sources. This approach may be most effective in turf. However, don't be fooled into thinking that if you eliminate grubs from the lawn, you also eliminate moles. A mole's diet consists of many other foods. Even if you manage to remove all food sources, moles may only move to

Coping With Dogs and Cats

Though dogs and cats may be wonderful deterrents to other animal pests, they can also become pests themselves in a garden. Dogs may wander through the garden, happily trampling or rolling on plants and digging just where you've planted. And cats seem to regard a freshly dug garden as an ideal litter box. How can you keep these pets from destroying your garden?

For dogs, the best solution is exclusion. If neighborhood dogs are out of control, a fence is the only workable method. Family pets can either be fenced out of an area or trained to stay out. Protect fragile individual plants by placing wire mesh around them.

Cats are harder to control. You can try luring them away from an area by planting catnip in a corner. Newly dug garden beds full of fluffy, loose dry soil are usually very attractive to cats. After a few waterings, the ground will become more tightly packed and will not be as attractive. For a stronger deterrent, try laying chicken wire over a newly planted bed. Be sure to remove the wire before the plants start to grow through it. Some gardeners recommend sprinkling red pepper or blocking the area where the cat crosses the fence with boards or wire.

There are some commercially available spray products that are said to discourage both cats and dogs. Mulches may also discourage both dogs and cats. Coarse mulches such as bark are particularly unpleasant for them. You can also set up a "forest" of kindling in a prized garden bed, but that may not be the garden design you want.

Often a house cat will prove to be adept at stalking a mole, even though the feline won't hunt it for food.

nearby areas and check your lawn periodically for food.

Predators   House cats are sometimes adept at mole control. Though not attracted to moles for food, cats with a strong hunting instinct often relish digging for moles as though it were a sport.

Trap crops   A new theory has emerged suggesting that moles can be kept at bay by developing a trap crop. The gardener designates an area of the garden as a mole garden. Here, the gardener stores, collects, or scatters compost material and keeps it moist. This in turn encourages earthworms, a favorite food of moles. The theory is that in time the moles will discover the easy pickings the gardener has provided and limit their digging to the trap-crop area.

Although trap crops sound like a charitable and generous alternative, a humane attempt at peaceful coexistence, there is no guarantee the animals will stay where you want them. In nature, an abundant food supply usually encourages animals to produce more offspring, which leads to a burgeoning population. Your resident moles will likely overrun the trap-crop area and disperse to other parts of your garden, creating a bigger problem than the one you start-

ed with. If you select trap crops as a strategy, do so with cautious optimism.

Ineffective methods   Through the years gardeners have tried to solve mole problems by placing in the tunnel system irritating materials such as rose branches, razor blades, broken glass, bleach, moth balls, lye, and even dead fish and human hair. They have also tinkered with frightening devices such as molewheels, vibrating windmills, whistles, and ultrasonic devices. In recent years it has been suggested that chewing gum can kill moles by causing intestinal blockage in those moles that ingest the gum.

Although studies have proved these methods worthless, many gardeners swear by them. However, there is a simple explanation for this supposed "success." Mole activity varies according to soil conditions and abundance of prey. Decreased mole activity, therefore, is due more probably to the mole's intermittent comings and goings than to a home remedy. This is not to say that gardeners haven't experienced success developing innovative ideas. Just because a method hasn't been substantiated by a scientific study doesn't mean it should be abandoned. Whichever method you choose, consider potential hazards to people, pets, and other nontarget animals and degradation of the environment.

POCKET GOPHERS

Gardeners in the West and the Midwest need little introduction to pocket gophers. No other mammal pest causes so much frustration and outright anger as does the pocket gopher. Gardeners in the East should consider themselves fortunate that they never have to deal with this fossorial rodent.

The correct term for the mammal is pocket gopher, so named because of its external fur-lined pouches on each cheek. Most gardeners, when they are not hurling unprintable epithets at these pests, simply refer to them as gophers. There is no other group of animal pests that will spark a livelier conversation among gardeners than pocket gophers.

All pocket gophers belong to the taxonomic family *Geomyidae*. Within the family there are 5 genera and 33 species. The species of con-cern to most gardeners are the plains, eastern, desert, and Texas pocket gophers (all in the genus *Geomys*); the eastern, western, southern, northern, and valley pocket gophers (genus *Thomomys*); and the yellow-faced pocket gopher (genus *Pappogeomys*).

Generally, pocket gophers are found west of the Mississippi River. However, eastern species occur as far east as Ohio and as far south as Florida. They are absent from the rest of the eastern seaboard. Only the *Thomomys* group extends into Canada.

Because all species are similar in appearance and habit, identifying individual species is not necessary in selecting control methods. However, if you are interested in learning which species is causing problems in your garden, contact your cooperative extension office or visit the public library.

Pocket gophers have long been considered the scourge of gardeners in the West and the Midwest.

Pocket Gopher Tunnel System

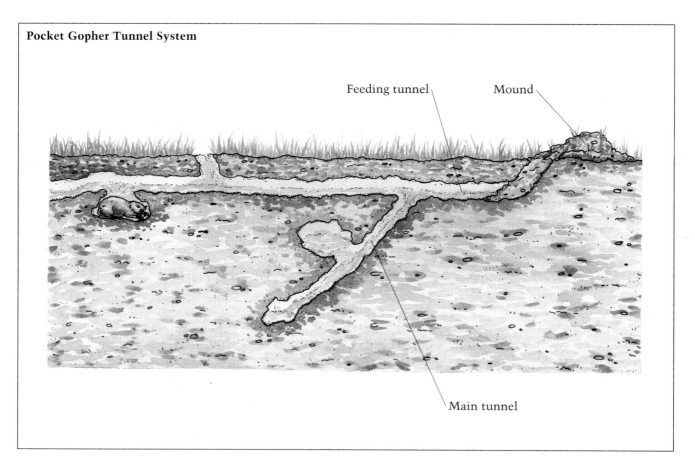

Feeding tunnel

Mound

Main tunnel

Description, Habit, and Habitat

Pocket gophers range in length from 5 to 12 inches. Their color may vary from light beige to various shades of brown to almost black. Pocket gophers use the external pouches on their cheeks as saddlebags to carry vegetable matter while walking, running, or digging throughout their tunnel systems.

Pocket gophers do not hibernate. They must cache enough food to maintain their basal metabolic rate throughout the year. Unlike moles, gophers are strict vegetarians. They prefer to eat roots, bulbs, tubers, corms, and the portions of plants found aboveground. It is hard to think of a plant pocket gophers do not eat. They feed on annuals, perennials, shrubs, trees, and turf. Pocket gophers, by feeding on the roots, have even killed large coniferous trees with a basal diameter in excess of 36 inches. They feed at any time throughout the day or night the year around.

Gophers are solitary animals, living by themselves in tunnel systems that cover their feeding area. They mate in late winter and early spring, and the young may be driven from the nest when they are just six weeks of age.

Damage Characteristics

Recognizing which species of gopher is causing garden problems is not necessary, but distinguishing between the pocket gopher and the mole is. The best way to differentiate between the two is by examining the type of mounds they make.

When a gopher digs its tunnel system it pushes the dirt from the burrow opening at a 45-degree angle to the soil surface, a small amount at a time. This produces a crescent-shaped mound. When finished, the gopher always plugs its hole with dirt. The plug is almost always visible when viewed from above. A mole produces a cone-shaped mound with no visible plug (see page 17). The presence or absence of the plug is one of the best field marks in helping you identify which animal is causing the problem. If you see a plug, you know you have a pocket gopher.

Gophers use their below-ground tunnel systems to get from one part of their territory to another. They live mostly below ground, subsisting on the subterranean portion of plants. However, they also forage for food aboveground, outside their tunnel system.

*A crescent shape and
the obviously visible
plug that seals the
mound characterize
a gopher mound.*

A gopher's tunnel system has many parts, including areas for nesting, food caches, and escape. In addition to the large mounds created through excavation, an individual burrow may have several smaller feeding tunnel openings. These openings give the animal access to plants aboveground, and are often seen in turf and ground covers. People sometimes confuse feeding tunnel openings with the diggings of field mice, voles, or even large insects. The best distinguishable characteristic is that gophers plug their burrow openings whereas the others do not.

Gopher traps, such as this box trap, are placed in the gopher tunnel, then covered with dirt.

Gopher Traps

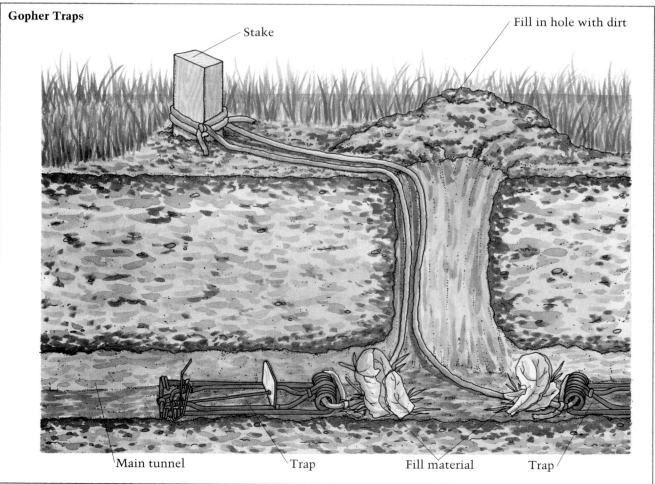

Stake

Fill in hole with dirt

Main tunnel   Trap   Fill material   Trap

The excavation of dirt, at either the large mounds or the feeding tunnels, is the only visible sign of pocket gopher activity. Unlike moles, which create surface runways as well as mounds, there are no other telltale signs that gophers are present.

Management and Prevention Strategies

Nearly all the methods for dealing with pocket gophers are lethal. Live traps are unavailable, and relocation would probably result in the gopher's death anyway. Removed from its burrow system, the only environment it knows, a gopher is helpless, unable to protect itself from predators or the elements. Exclusion through fencing is the only effective nonlethal control.

Trapping   Kill traps are the most effective means of removing pocket gophers. There are two types of gopher traps: wire and box. Both are available at hardware stores, garden supply stores, or nurseries. You will have to decide which type best suits your needs and stick with it. As with all trapping, practice and patience are required to achieve success.

Most common wire traps are similar in design and function and are generally easy to set and use. They create less soil disturbance than do box traps, and are easier to carry when setting several of them. Check with store personnel for the best choice for your situation.

The common box traps are similar in design, although some are made of wood while others are made of plastic. These traps are larger than the wire traps and therefore create more soil disturbance when you are setting them. Again, check with store personnel for the best choice for your needs.

Before setting the trap you must first probe the gopher runway the same way you do for moles (see page 19). Like mole traps, gopher traps are not baited and are set in the path of the animal. Since you cannot know from which direction the gopher will approach the trap, it is important to set two traps in the tunnel system, pointed in opposite directions.

Once you have located the tunnel, dig into the tunnel to place the traps. Be sure to wear gloves when handling the traps. Set the traps well within the tunnel to increase the chances of the gopher tripping the mechanism. Before setting them, attach a piece of string, twine, or wire to the rear of each trap and extend the piece aboveground. This will allow you to pull out the traps without having to search through the soil with your hand.

Once you have set the traps, take extra care to ensure that light and air do not enter through the opening you have dug. Place a wadded sheet of newspaper or other similar material behind the trap, taking care not to cover it. Some type of edible forage used as wadding—lettuce, cole crops, carrot tops—increases your chances of catching the animal. Gently fill the rest of the hole with soil. The wadding prevents dirt from covering the trap and rendering it inoperable.

Check traps daily by opening the hole and pulling on the string, twine, or wire you attached to the rear of the trap. If the trap is sprung and no animal is inside, reset it and repeat the procedure. Though this may prove tedious, it is usually worth the effort. Since gophers are territorial they normally check their tunnel system daily. This habit improves your chance of success.

If you have caught the animal, fill the hole with dirt and place your trap into another runway system. Because pocket gophers are solitary animals, there is no need to retrap in the same tunnel system. Bury the animal in the tunnel or contact your local wildlife resource agency for other legal disposal methods.

Baiting   Baiting is an effective alternative for controlling pocket gophers. Always read the label directions before using toxic baits. Follow all safety precautions.

Most pocket gopher baits are based on either small loose grains or manufactured grain-based pellets that have the toxicant incorporated into the product. Originally formulated using only strychnine alkaloid as the toxicant, pocket gopher baits now contain different acute toxicants or anticoagulant chemicals. Some of the anticoagulants may require multiple applications. To be effective, toxic bait must be presented fresh. Old, moldy, or stale baits are unappetizing to pocket gophers.

Pocket gopher baits are applied below ground, where gophers forage. Never use them aboveground. If you do, you may accidentally poison a child or nontarget animal.

To find the burrow, use the same probing technique for setting a trap. Remove the probe

Use a probe, such as this commercial variety or a homemade one, to locate the gopher tunnel before placing bait.

once you have located the burrow. Apply a teaspoon of toxic bait with a measuring spoon into the hole you created with the probe. Use the measuring spoon for applying bait only! After baiting, close the hole with a dirt clod, rock, newspaper, wood, or any other available material. As with setting traps, it is very important to prevent light or air from entering the burrow and alerting the animal of a disturbance. To ensure maximum efficiency you should bait at least two sites within the same burrow system.

If you are dealing with one or two animals in your garden, placing the bait in this way is a sound approach. However, if your garden is an acre or more, or if you have a number of animals causing problems, you may want to consider purchasing a bait applicator.

Most bait applicators include a probe with a handle and foot rest, which simplify probing the soil, and a triggered bait reservoir. Once you find the burrow, you need only to pull the trigger, and the applicator automatically places

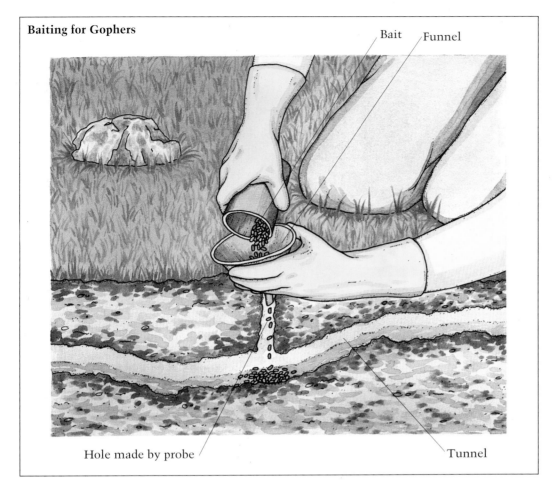

Baiting for Gophers

Bait

Funnel

Hole made by probe

Tunnel

a predetermined amount of bait in the runway. Most applicators have a reservoir capable of holding a pound or more of bait. These machines greatly enhance your ability to treat several burrow systems in much less time.

For gardens of five acres or more there is available an artificial burrow builder and bait applicator. This machine is pulled by a tractor with 50 horsepower or greater. It creates an artificial burrow that intersects the gopher's burrow system and automatically distributes toxic grain bait at equal intervals. The machine is designed to take advantage of the solitary and aggressive behavior of pocket gophers. The resident gopher perceives the artificial burrow as a threat from another animal and when investigating, encounters the toxic bait.

Fumigants Fumigating the burrow system with sulfur compound smoke bombs has the same shortcomings as those mentioned in conjunction with moles (see page 20). The pungent smell of the burning compounds alerts gophers to the impending threat, and they respond by plugging off the tunnel. Study the label directions before using. Severe burns and gas fires can occur if these devices are improperly handled.

Some gardeners also devise their own fumigation systems, similar to those used for moles and ground squirrels (see pages 20 and 42).

Flooding Place a garden hose into the main runway and leave it on for several minutes to force the pocket gopher from its burrow. Use a shovel, hoe, or pitchfork to dispatch the animal when it escapes from the tunnel. Do not catch the animal with your hands, and wear gloves for added protection. Pocket gophers can inflict severe bites and sever a finger.

Exclusion Many gardeners have had success using fencing underground and making wire baskets to protect raised beds or specific plants. A great deal of work is required to place a wire mesh barrier in an existing garden, but the task is relatively simple if the mesh is incorporated into the early stages of garden development.

Protecting a Raised Bed

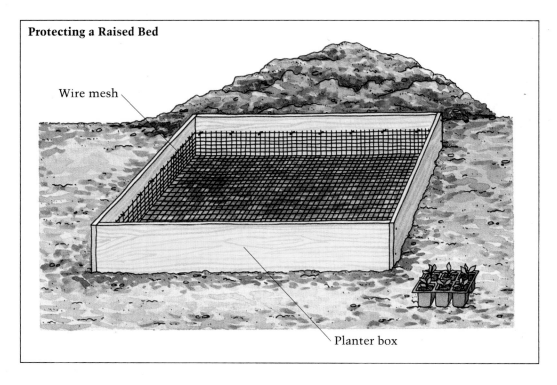

Wire mesh

Planter box

Mesh Basket Around Roots

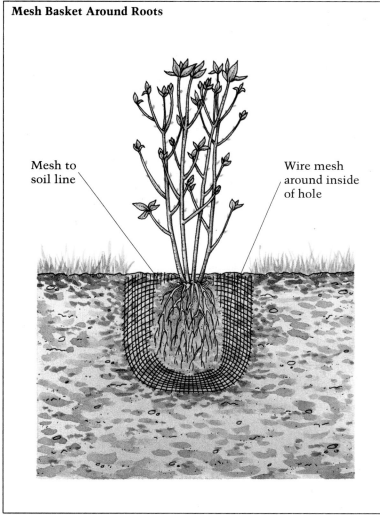

Mesh to soil line

Wire mesh around inside of hole

The size of the wire mesh must be big enough so that it does not inhibit root development and water penetration. However, it must be small enough to keep gophers from passing through the openings. A mesh size ½ inch in diameter is adequate for all pocket gopher species found in North America. The wire should be galvanized to ensure an extended period of protection. Alternative materials such as nylon mesh, though easier to work with, are not strong enough to stop pocket gophers.

To protect a larger tree or shrub, apply the same concept of root protection only on a smaller scale. Wire mesh fashioned like a basket can protect the roots of trees if the baskets are in place at the time of planting. After you have dug the hole for the tree or shrub, line it with the mesh. Then complete the planting of the tree or shrub.

A test conducted at the University of California at Davis proved that perimeter fencing alone does not keep pocket gophers out of an area. In the test a perimeter fence was buried 4 feet into the soil and extended 3 feet aboveground. Pocket gophers dug below the 4-foot barrier. They also surprised researchers by climbing over the aboveground portion of the fence.

Frightening devices   A number of sonic devices, both electronic and mechanical, produce a variety of frightening noises such as squeaks, rattles, whistles, and other high-frequency ultrasonic waves. Laboratory tests conducted at the University of California at Davis have proved that they are ineffective. Most pocket gophers are exposed to a myriad of raucous noisemakers such as lawn mowers, sprinklers, rotary tillers, and children and are not repelled by them. Because pocket gophers depend on their tunnel systems for survival, an annoying sound is not sufficient cause to leave an area or abandon a burrow.

Some gardeners have also reported success with plantings that discourage gophers. The aptly named gopher spurge plant (*Euphorbia lathyris*) is said to repel both gophers and moles. However, these claims have not been substantiated. The stem of this plant is poisonous and can burn skin and eyes.

The smell of gopher spurge (Euphorbia lathyris) *is said to keep gophers at bay.*

Above- and Below-Ground Pests

These versatile animals are equally at home above and below the soil surface.

Woodchucks, ground squirrels, chipmunks, rabbits, and voles are common animal pests that are well adapted to life above the soil surface. Although they all bear their young and hide from danger in below-ground tunnels or dens, they forage above as well as below. Woodchucks, ground squirrels, chipmunks, and voles are closely related, all belonging to the order *Rodentia.* Rabbits belong to the order *Lagomorpha.* It is possible to find a representative from each group in the same area.

This chapter will help you recognize and minimize the damage associated with each group. Keep in mind that there are multiple species of woodchucks, ground squirrels, chipmunks, rabbits, and voles. Fortunately, most species are found in certain geographic regions and do not overlap much. If you are interested in determining which species is trespassing in your yard, contact your cooperative extension office.

Many of the solutions for controlling damage are similar for each group of animal pests. If you are having problems with more than one pest, you may find that combining several strategies is more effective than using only one.

Some animal pests, such as this young woodchuck, are equally at home above the ground and below it.

Woodchucks (Marmota monax) *can be found across North America from Alaska through Canada and throughout the eastern United States.*

WOODCHUCKS

Gardeners in the United States and Canada have a variety of names for this critter: woodchuck, chuck, groundhog, whistle pig, siffleur, rockchuck, and marmot. Generally, the term marmot is used for the western species while the terms woodchuck, groundhog, and chuck are used for the eastern species. But it should be emphasized that woodchucks and groundhogs are the same animal.

This animal pest comprises three distinct groups: the woodchuck (*Marmota monax*), the yellow-bellied marmot (*M. flaviventris*), and the hoary marmot (*M. caligata*).

In general, members of the woodchuck group are found from Alaska through Canada and throughout the eastern United States. Yellow-bellied marmots inhabit the mountainous regions of the West. Hoary marmots are found throughout the Pacific Northwest. In all, there are 34 recognized subspecies of woodchucks.

Description, Habit, and Habitat

Woodchucks are heavy-bodied rodents that can weigh from 4 to 24 pounds. They have short legs and are very good diggers. The color of their fur varies from gray to brownish yellow, the underside being a slightly lighter shade.

Woodchucks are true hibernators, spending a good part of their lives below ground in suspended animation. They are able to sustain themselves during hibernation from fat reserves they accumulated while active. In some areas of the country, chucks hibernate for as much as three or four months of the year.

Most woodchucks breed at two years of age. Some species are capable of reproducing only every other year. The gestation period is about 32 days, the young born in early spring. The average litter size is four to six young.

Woodchucks are mainly crepuscular, which means they are active during twilight and just before dawn. Pure vegetarians attracted to a

Butternut squash satisfies the vegetarian appetite of a woodchuck.

Woodchucks generally place their burrows near observation points, such as this old stone foundation.

wide variety of forage crops, they favor beans, peas, other legumes, carrot tops, alfalfa, clover, and grasses.

Woodchucks cause significant damage in gardens, nurseries, orchards, and farms. Signs of their depredation in gardens and farms are obvious: One woodchuck can consume up to 1½ pounds of vegetation every 24 hours. Less conspicuous in nurseries and orchards is the harm they inflict on fruit trees and ornamen-

tals by their gnawing and clawing. The large mounds of dirt they produce from digging pose a hazard to equipment, livestock, and horse-back riders.

These powerful diggers prefer habitats with dry soil. They live in open woodland, thickets, rocky slopes, and crop fields. An important feature of their habitat is an observation point such as a fence post or rock outcropping from which they can survey an area.

Management and Prevention Strategies

When deciding on management strategies for woodchucks, you must first choose between lethal and nonlethal methods. Before applying any lethal methods, check with your cooperative extension office to ascertain whether it is legal to kill woodchucks in your area.

Exclusion   Fencing is a nonlethal alternative that can provide long-term protection while easing the conscience of those gardeners who oppose killing wildlife or who enjoy watching woodchucks from afar. Two types of fencing—standard and electric—are the most effective for keeping woodchucks away and can be adapted to meet your needs.

Standard fencing should be constructed of a material that won't allow woodchucks to climb through the fence or over the top. Woodchucks are good climbers and can easily scale wire fences. If you plan to use wire, you must block the woodchuck aboveground as well as below. To do so, first bend the bottom of the wire out-ward so that about a foot of wire lies along the ground. Cover this extension with about an inch of soil. This will discourage the woodchuck from digging under the fence right where it meets the ground. At the top, extend the wire a couple of feet above the fence posts and bend it slightly outward. If a woodchuck tries to climb, it will bend the fence under its weight and will not be able to make it over the top.

If you choose wooden fencing, be sure to bury the bottom about 12 inches below the ground to prevent animals from burrowing underneath. The fence aboveground should be at least 4 feet tall to prevent woodchucks from jumping or climbing over the top.

Electric fencing also provides a protective barrier. Retrofit an existing fence by placing a single strand of electrified wire on plastic extenders about 4 or 5 inches from the fence and an equal distance from the ground. This wire will prevent climbing or burrowing. Electric fencing will not harm the woodchuck or any other animal. The low amperage provides just enough of a shock to startle and discourage.

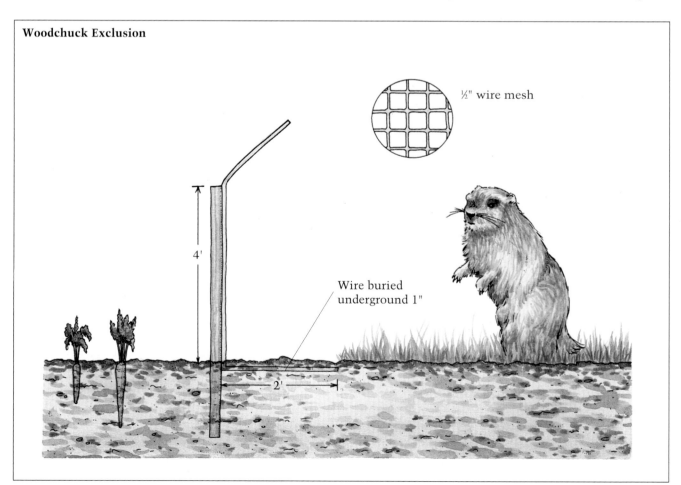

Woodchuck Exclusion

½" wire mesh

4'

Wire buried underground 1"

2'

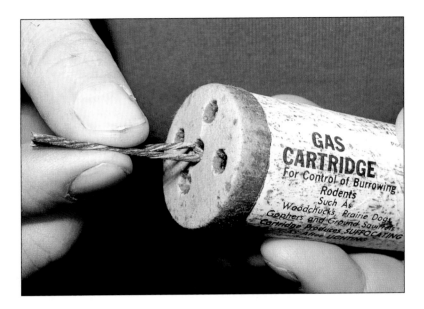

Top: When lighting a gas cartridge, double the fuse before inserting it into the cartridge.
Center: Light the end of the fuse before inserting it into the ground.
Bottom: Once lit, place the fuse in the ground and cover it with dirt.

A word of caution: Before working on the fence, always check the power source to be sure that is turned off.

Repellents A good deal of research is currently being conducted on repellents that discourage chucks from feeding on specific plants. The challenge is to develop repellents that pose no danger to nontargets such as humans and pets and to the plants that are to be protected. You can expect to see more nonlethal repellents available by the end of the century.

Many people have developed home remedies that may be useful in repelling woodchucks and other rodents. One such remedy, a mixture of cayenne pepper, water, and cooking oil, may provide short-term relief when sprayed on plants.

Trapping Live traps are effective in removing woodchucks and reducing damage. Before deciding on trapping, be sure to check state and local regulations. Many states and communities, for example, have placed restrictions on releasing animals from live traps in an attempt to prevent the spread of disease.

Live traps are available from agricultural supply stores and mail-order suppliers. Cage-type live traps for woodchucks should be at least 10 inches × 24 inches. Two-door traps should be at least 10 inches × 10 inches × 30 inches.

Place live traps near the burrow entrance and bait them with apples, carrot tops, or lettuce. Check the traps twice daily. If a woodchuck is captured, release it according to state or local regulations.

Baiting There are no poisons legally registered for controlling woodchucks. It is unwise to concoct poisons of your own because to do so may be illegal and because they may be potent enough to kill children and family pets.

Fumigants The most common lethal control for woodchucks is the gas cartridge. These slow-burning, cylindrical cartridges are ignited and then placed into the burrow opening. The burning cartridge produces carbon monoxide, which accumulates in the burrow and kills the woodchuck. To maximize the effectiveness of gas cartridges, you must first seal all but one burrow opening with soil to prevent the gas from escaping. Then place the gas cartridge in

Your choices in eliminating woodchucks range from lethal methods to simply altering your garden habitat so that it no longer encourages them to enter it.

the one remaining opening, pushing it deep into the tunnel. Seal the opening with soil to prevent the gas from escaping.

Gas cartridges are usually available at agricultural supply stores. Study the label directions before using an incendiary device. Severe burns and grass fires can occur if these devices are improperly handled. For more information on using these fumigants, see page 20.

Shooting This method is effective if all safety precautions are followed. Obviously, shooting is practical only in rural areas. Before deciding on shooting woodchucks, be sure to check state hunting regulations.

Habitat alterations Because woodchucks have specific habitat needs, altering their habitats sometimes discourages them from becoming pests in your garden. Remove any materials that can serve as an observation platform, such as rock piles, barren fence posts, sunning platforms, tree stumps, and rock walls.

GROUND SQUIRRELS

Ground squirrels, like woodchucks, are rodents. However, ground squirrels are more gregarious than woodchucks and are found in large numbers and colonies. In the West ground squirrels can become a serious pest of gardens, parks, rangeland, and farms.

The ground squirrel is known by a variety of names. Some of the more common are gopher, picket pin, spermophile, antelope squirrel, prairie squirrel, and rock squirrel. In North America there are 22 recognized species and 93 subspecies, not including chipmunks. Ground squirrels belong to one of two genera, *Ammospermophilus* or *Spermophilus* (formerly known as *Citellus*).

Description, Habit, and Habitat

Ground squirrels are active and alert during the day. They have short rounded ears and conspicuous eyes, and the color of their fur is various shades of brown, with a yellow wash. One of the most colorful and striking species is the

Dealing With Skunks

Skunks have often been depicted in movies and children's books as lovable and delicate creatures. In reality, they are wild animals that have evolved into one of nature's most adaptable species. They are equipped with a powerful and protective scent gland that produces a potentially dangerous liquid that can be shot as far as 10 feet!

Skunks, which can be found throughout the United States and Canada, are primarily nocturnal, though some can be seen in early morning and evening hours. They are generalists, feeding on insects, eggs, small animals, and discarded food found in compost piles and garbage cans. They relish dog and cat foods. Most damage caused to garden plants is through their digging in search of grubs, worms, and other soil inhabitants.

The best deterrent to skunks in the garden is exclusion and prevention. Remove all pet foods from outside at night. Surround your garden with a 2-foot-high wire mesh or picket fence and screen all openings beneath your house or outbuilding. Do not place table scraps in your compost pile or in open garbage receptacles. Collect fallen and rotting fruit from below trees.

If a skunk should take up residence beneath a porch or patio, do not try to trap it yourself. Skunks are dangerous. They not only produce a scent that can cause temporary blindness, but they also are a primary source of rabies. They should only be handled by a professional who has experience with them (in most areas, it is illegal for residents to trap and relocate skunks). If you are having problems with skunks living on your property, contact your local wildlife resource agency for advice and assistance. You can also check for private pest control businesses that deal with skunks in your local telephone directory under "Pest Control."

If your pets have been sprayed by a skunk, to neutralize the smell, wash the pets with diluted vinegar, tomato juice, or neutroleum alpha.

This Columbian ground squirrel is native to the Pacific Northwest. The large, conspicuous entrance hole is typical of ground squirrels burrows.

13-lined ground squirrel (*S. tridecemlineatus*) of the plains states.

Ground squirrels are highly adaptable. It is believed that humans, by converting prairie and rangeland to cropland, have enhanced the environment in favor of ground squirrels. Alterations of the environment have allowed some species of ground squirrel to expand their home range. For example, the 13-lined squirrel is a prairie native whose current range now includes Michigan, Wisconsin, Indiana, Illinois, and Ohio. Much of this range expansion has occurred since 1900.

All ground squirrels hibernate. They may also estivate. Estivation is a form of torpor similar to hibernation that occurs during summer. You need to be aware of these behaviors and make an effort to document the time in which they occur in your region. Knowing these time periods helps you make the most of management efforts when the animals are active.

Depending on climatic conditions, ground squirrel activity generally begins in February and continues into September or early October. Usually, the males are active one or two weeks before the females and breeding takes place shortly after the females emerge. The male ground squirrel breeds with more than one female. Ground squirrels generally reproduce only once a year, the young born in the early spring. Depending on the species, litter size may vary from 2 to 10 pups.

Damage Characteristics

Ground squirrels are omnivorous, eating grasshoppers, ants, leafy vegetables, seeds, lizards, and even other rodent species. A study in southern Nevada found that the white-tailed antelope squirrel eats not only lizards, which account for nearly half of its diet, but also six genera of rodents.

The food habits of these animals may change seasonally. It is not uncommon for some species to feed primarily on leafy vegetable matter in spring, then alter their diets to include insects, seeds, and fruits in summer. If given the opportunity, many species feed on the young of small birds, including their eggs.

You should not let the term ground squirrel mislead you into thinking that these animals are incapable of climbing. The California ground squirrel, *S. beecheyi,* is adept at reaching fruit and nuts far above the ground—and damaging the trees they climb.

To the gardener ground squirrels can become quite a nuisance. If left undisturbed, they can swell in number quickly and plunder all available aboveground forage. They prefer cereal and grain crops, legumes, almonds, walnuts, and row crops. In drier habitats, ground squirrels damage irrigation systems by gnawing on hoses and tubing to reach the water inside.

Their burrowing and insatiable digging can increase soil erosion, damage garden and farm equipment, destroy levies and dikes, and pose a threat to hikers and horseback riders. In most states ground squirrels are considered nongame animals and can be taken at any time. To be on the safe side, however, you should check with local authorities for regulations regarding ground squirrel removal.

In the West, ground squirrels are potential carriers of the flea *Diamanus montanus,* which transmits the bacterium that causes bubonic plague. If you live in the West and witness a sudden die-off of ground squirrels in your area, you should notify local health officials.

Management and Prevention Strategies

Ground squirrels are not a species that can easily be dealt with using nonlethal methods. For example, if you catch a ground squirrel live you may have difficulty obtaining permission to release it on someone else's property. Because of their incessant digging, ground squirrels are a species few people want in their yard. In the West, because of the threat they pose as vectors of plague, few land managers will risk liability by allowing the relocation of ground squirrels on public lands. For this reason, it is actually illegal to release ground squirrels on public lands in some western states.

Exclusion The only effective nonlethal control option is exclusion. Fences provide some

protection from ground squirrels if you choose the proper materials. Wire mesh or woven wire designs are ineffective because ground squirrels are good climbers. Wooden fences 4 to 6 feet high are a better deterrent. As you would for woodchucks, bury wooden fences at least 12 inches below the soil surface to discourage burrowing underneath.

Electric fences can also be an effective impediment for ground squirrels. Follow the directions given for woodchucks (see page 36).

Trapping If fewer than six ground squirrels are a problem in your garden, then lethal trapping may an appropriate method of control. Two types of traps are effective on ground squirrels: the box trap and the large-size snap trap. Both are available at agricultural supply stores and at some nurseries and hardware stores. These traps work best if placed near a burrow or tunnel entrance.

A number of baits work well for ground squirrels, but they seem to prefer walnuts, almonds, oats, and barley. Place the bait behind the trigger or attach it to the trigger mecha-

Chipmunks not only feed on garden crops, they also damage plants and bulbs as they dig for food.

A live trap will let you capture squirrels without killing them, but these traps are often unavailable and relocating ground squirrels is difficult.

nism. It is best to place the bait near the traps for several days but not to set the traps. This allows the animals to accustom themselves to the new objects in their territory. After the squirrels have become comfortable with taking the bait, rebait and set the traps.

Fumigants Many states require that you obtain special permits or licenses before using certain fumigants. Gas cartridges generally do not require special permits and can be effective on ground squirrels. Follow the same procedure as you would for woodchucks (see page 37). If you are using a sulfur-type smoke bomb, take care not to start a fire or burn your skin. As with any fumigant, check first with local agricultural or wildlife officials for special restrictions in your area.

Gardeners must realize that ground squirrel burrows can be extensive. If you are using a fumigant, you must seal all cracks and entrances, except the one to be treated, so that the toxic gas cannot escape. Fumigants are not effective during hibernation and estivation because the squirrels plug themselves into their burrows with soil at these times. Plugging inhibits the penetration of smoke and gases throughout the tunnel system.

Some gardeners use carbon monoxide gas from an engine to fumigate rodent burrows. To do this, attach a length of garden hose to the

Gassing a Ground Squirrel

Hole to burrow

exhaust pipe of any small engine such as a lawn mower or rotary tiller. Place the other end of the hose into the burrow opening, and push soil around the hose to seal the opening. After checking the rest of the tunnel system for possible leaks, start the engine. Never use engine exhaust near houses or other buildings. Escaping gases can kill people and pets if concentrations accumulate in enclosed areas.

Baiting By far the most effective control, toxic baits are available at nurseries and agricultural supply stores. You should purchase just enough toxic bait for one treatment for two reasons. First, animal pests respond better to fresh bait. Second, there is less chance of accidental poisoning when little or no bait lingers after an application.

Before using toxic bait, precondition ground squirrels to accept a nontoxic bait such as apples, oats, or nuts. Wait for a couple of days or until the squirrels have found the food supply and regularly visit the site to eat. Then replace the nontoxic bait with the toxic bait. Leave the toxic bait out for only about 24 hours. Removing the toxic bait at a prescribed time diminishes the chance of poisoning a nontarget animal. After you have removed the treated bait, evaluate your success. If you have properly prebaited and conditioned the animals to

feed at your bait station, you should see as much as a 90 percent reduction in the number of squirrels. If some squirrels are left, repeat the entire procedure but use a different toxic bait. Research has shown that squirrels prefer some baits over others. Alternating toxicants helps ground squirrels overcome their shyness of bait as well as improves your control efforts.

Gardeners should be sensitive to the environmental fate of all pesticides. To minimize the spread of toxic baits and the exposure of nontarget species to them, consider using a bait station in a specific location. Bait stations can be made of old tires sawed in half (be careful not to saw steel-belted tires—they are very rough on saw blades), 4-inch clothes-drier ducting, and 4-inch plastic or rubber irrigation or drain piping cut into 18- to 24-inch lengths. They must be constructed to hold approximately two pounds of treated bait. These stations, which can be used for both toxic and nontoxic baits, also protect bait from the elements.

Before using any baits, check with local authorities for their legal status.

Habitat alterations Once you have removed ground squirrels from your area, take quick steps to destroy all tunnel and burrow systems so that the animals will not return. Research has proved that ground squirrels disperse from neighboring sites to reinvade burrows. Newly arriving squirrels can perceive the presence of the old systems from the scent left by their predecessors. Complete destruction of the system through discing, plowing, or rototilling removes the scent. Merely filling in the systems with dirt is not so effective.

CHIPMUNKS

Chipmunks, small relatives of the larger ground squirrels, are considered garden pests throughout much of the eastern United States. The species of greatest concern is the eastern chipmunk, *Tamias striatus*. Although chipmunks are usually found in mature woodland, they can also inhabit other rural and suburban areas. They are most commonly seen around ornamental plantings, rock piles, outbuildings, and below patios and building foundations.

Chipmunks are one of the few species of wildlife that most people can easily recognize. The animals are entertaining to watch, and their antics can often bring hours of enjoyment.

Mountain Beavers of the Pacific Northwest

Locally known as boomers, these rodents of the coniferous forests in the Pacific Northwest can sometimes cause problems in the garden. *Aplodontia rufa* is the oldest-known rodent occurring in North America, its fossil record going back to the Pleistocene epoch. It is an opportunistic vegetarian that feeds on the tops of ferns, greens, and bulbs. A secretive animal, it prefers to stay in dense undergrowth found in second-growth stands of conifers, or in ditch banks where soil drainage is good.

To remove mountain beavers, consider cutting back vegetation that may be harboring them. Create a buffer zone, 25 to 50 feet wide, between your garden and adjacent mountain beaver habitat.

If damage continues, consult with local forestry officials for other options.

However, they can also wreak havoc in a garden setting, especially when they become numerous.

Description, Habit, and Habitat

The eastern chipmunk is a small, brownish animal 5 to 6 inches long, with two pale brown and five blackish strips down its back and two pale brown and two brownish strips on each side of its face. The rump is reddish brown. The tail is 3 to 4 inches long and covered with fur. A full-grown chipmunk weighs between 2 and 4 ounces. Chipmunks have a varied diet of nuts, berries, and seeds. They also consume mushrooms, insects, and even carrion if these are available.

Chipmunk burrows are often well concealed near buildings, garages, old tree stumps, and wood or brush piles. The burrow entrance is about 2 inches in diameter. Unlike the burrows of moles and pocket gophers, there are no obvious mounds around the entrance of a chipmunk burrow. The chipmunk carries the dirt in

The eastern chipmunk, Tamias striatus, *is fun to watch, but can wreak havoc on a garden.*

its cheek pouches and scatters it on the ground away from the burrow to make the entrance less conspicuous.

In most cases, the main tunnel is between 20 and 30 feet long. However, the complexity and the length of the tunnel system are often determined by the amount of cover and availability of food. A tunnel system will normally include a nest chamber, one or two food storage chambers, various tunnels connecting the main tunnel, and separate escape tunnels.

Chipmunks are generally solitary animals protective of their territories. Only during courtship and raising young are many chipmunks found together. Mating occurs twice a year, in early spring and in summer or early fall. Gestation is 31 days, and the young are usually born in early May and from August through October. Two to five young are born in each litter. Chipmunks become sexually mature in one year. The life expectancy for the eastern chipmunk is about three years.

The average territory of an adult chipmunk varies from a quarter acre to a half acre. Neighboring chipmunks often have overlapping territories. If sufficient food and cover are available, chipmunk densities can reach 10 animals per acre. The best time to observe chipmunk activity is in the early morning and late afternoon.

With the onset of cold weather chipmunks enter into a restless sleep in late fall or early winter and then hibernate for the rest of the winter. Most chipmunks emerge from hibernation by early March.

Damage Characteristics

Chipmunks cause damage by burrowing and feeding. Their burrowing destroys building foundations, concrete patios, retaining walls, and sidewalks. Their digging ruins flower and bulb plantings as they search for bulbs, seeds, garden fruits, and other plants to eat.

Management and Prevention Strategies

Prevention is usually the main goal of gardeners wishing to limit chipmunk damage. Several strategies are available to home gardeners.

Exclusion   The best method for managing chipmunk damage is to exclude them from the garden. If small beds of plants need protection, cover them with garden netting. If you think the animals may burrow beneath the garden netting, also bury hardware cloth below the plants at planting time.

Trapping   Many garden experts consider trapping the most practical method for removing chipmunks. Both live traps and common rat snap traps can be used.

Several effective baits for live-catching chipmunks include nuts, pumpkin and sunflower seeds, raisins, prune slices, and many breakfast

Patience is essential for trapping chipmunks, such as this one caught in a live trap. Prebaiting will condition an animal to approach a trap for food.

cereal grains. Place the live trap in a runway where you see chipmunks frequently, using the same methods as for moles and gophers. Prebaiting the site (see page 41) improves your chances of catching them. Check the trap daily once set. Release any unwanted animals caught in the traps, avoiding contact with them unless they are pets. Release live chipmunks several miles away from the point of capture, in a location where they will not become a problem for someone else. Also avoid contact with them.

Use the same baits for rat snap traps. As with live trapping, it is best to condition the animals by prebaiting.

Set the snap traps perpendicular to the chipmunk's runway or in pairs along the travel routes with the triggers facing away from each other. You can also place traps inside cardboard boxes with 2-inch-diameter holes cut into their ends. This will protect birds from being caught in the trap. Use snap traps only if they can be isolated from children, pets, or other wildlife.

Baiting   There are no poison baits available for homeowners to use against chipmunks.

Shooting   Shoot chipmunks as a last resort, and only where it is both legal and safe. The best time to find the animals is early on a bright sunny morning.

RABBITS
Few people, including children, need a detailed description to recognize a rabbit. In North America rabbits are collectively called cottontails. They are a separate species from hares.

Description, Habit, and Habitat
Rabbits can be found throughout the United States and southern Canada. They nest in burrows or warrens that have been abandoned by other animals such as woodchucks. Rabbits generally venture out only in morning and late afternoon and rarely travel more than a few acres. Rabbits are born in underground nests in an altricial state—eyes closed, hairless, unable to walk, and dependent on the mother for care and protection. They are weaned in about two weeks. They remain with the female for some time before venturing out on their own in search of their own territories.

Cottontails rely on agility rather than speed alone to escape predators. That is why you often see cottontails on roads, trails, walkways, or paths adjacent to brambles or other shrubs. They venture out into open areas during dawn and dusk to forage, but seldom do they stray far from cover. If frightened, they quickly return to the protective cover offered by the vegetation. Hedge rows and densely planted woody shrubs next to a food source such as your garden provide excellent rabbit habitat.

Damage caused by rabbits can be identified by the diagonal 45-degree cut made on a limb or sapling. Remember that in winter the snow level will allow rabbits to reach higher onto a tree or shrub for food.

Damage Characteristics

Unless you actually see rabbits feeding in your garden it is easy to confuse their browsing damage with that caused by deer. Most rabbits feed near ground level, except during winter, when hardened snow allows them to climb to food that is normally out of reach.

Rabbits feed on small shrubs, small woody trees (particularly conifers) less than ¼-inch in diameter, fruit-tree bark, turf, vegetables, and some flowers. Their cutting behavior on trees and shrubs is often an identifying characteristic. Rabbits make a diagonal 45-degree cut with their incisor teeth by turning their heads sideways to situate their teeth at the proper angle to clip the limb or sapling. Large browsers, like deer, don't have upper incisors, so they must tug on their food to break it off, resulting in a curlicue appearance at the chewed end of the plant material.

Most rabbits prefer leafy vegetation when it is available in spring and summer, but during winter they gnaw and girdle woody trees. It is during winter when damage is most likely to occur on fruit trees and woody ornamentals, including conifers. Rabbits can clip branches up to ¼ inch in diameter, making young planted trees susceptible to their feeding.

Management and Prevention Strategies

Although rabbits frustrate gardeners, many find them appealing and are reluctant to kill them. Fortunately, one of the best control approaches is exclusion from the garden, which leaves rabbits healthy and alive, free to forage elsewhere.

Exclusion Rabbits are not good climbers, so barriers do not have to be high. A fence 3 feet high, made of 2- or 3-inch woven wire mesh or other closely spaced grid and bent outward at the bottom, is adequate for deterring rabbits. Some fencing material is sold with wire mesh that gradually increases in size (see illustration on page 48). Place the more closely spaced mesh on the bottom to prevent smaller animals from entering the garden. Generally they do not try to dig underneath or jump over a barrier of these dimensions. If you live in an area that receives snow in winter, be sure the fence clears the snow line by 3 feet.

The protective cover offered by vegetation provides a natural habitat for wild rabbits.

A fence made of lightweight material such as nylon mesh is easy to move if you choose not to construct a permanent barrier around the entire garden. This allows you to purchase relatively small amounts of material, minimize costs, and selectively protect plants.

If individual trees need protection, construct a cylindrical fence using poultry wire around the base of the tree. The enclosure needs to be approximately 3 feet high and 10 to 12 inches away from the tree. This is an effective way to protect fruit trees and young conifers from winter feeding.

Repellents   Commercially available repellents must be applied often because they are susceptible to climatic conditions. The most effective repellent available is thiram (tetramethyl-thiuram-disulfide), which is intended to minimize gnawing of trunks and limbs. If a small area or specific plant needs protection, exclusion offers a more permanent solution.

Trapping   To live trap, first identify the runway that rabbits use often. Bait the trap with lettuce, carrots, or beet tops and then set it in the runway. If the runway is the main entry point into your garden, the animals will often walk directly into the trap. This method may work well even when the traps are unbaited. Live trap size 3 or 4 is sufficient. Purchase live traps through farm catalogs, agricultural supply stores, and mail-order sources, or rent them from the local humane society.

Rabbit Fencing

Live trapping presents the problem of relocating rabbits as well as the potential for disease transmission. If you decide to trap, first consult with local authorities for rules and restrictions. When dealing with trapped rabbits, wear protective clothing, particularly gloves.

Frightening devices　Gardeners have tried countless methods to frighten away browsing rabbits. Metallic flashing, rattles, noisemakers, and scarecrows have all been used with varying degrees of success. Most commercial frightening devices do a poor job at best because rabbits usually become accustomed to the device shortly after installation. Shouting and waving your arms usually gets their attention and causes them to run away, but only for as long as you are around. You would do better to consider a barking dog.

Shooting　As with other garden pests, shooting rabbits is an option only where it is safe and legal to do so. Cottontails are regulated under state fish and game codes. Check local regulations before taking rabbits. If you choose to shoot rabbits, you may want to consider hunting them for food rather than discarding them.

Habitat alterations　It is possible to make rabbits voluntarily locate to another area by altering or removing their habitat. Because rabbits need protective cover for escape routes, consider the removal of brambles and other dense, woody vegetation if your garden is surrounded by them. If there is no cover, there will be no rabbits. In combination with fencing this is effective and nonlethal. Keep in mind, however, that by removing protective cover, you also greatly decrease bird habitat and the presence of birds in your garden.

Left: Individual trees can be protected from rabbit damage by encasing the trunks in poultry wire.
Right: Setting a trap in the runway or path used by rabbits is often effective. Here, tracks in the snow provide a good clue as to the path the invading rabbits will take.

Though tiny, voles, or meadow mice, can inflict considerable damage on vegetables, such as this artichoke.

VOLES

The vole is an indigenous rodent that is a member of the genus *Microtus*. It is known by a host of names: meadow vole, meadow mouse, field mouse, and microtine.

Though voles are called meadow mice, in many ways they resemble young pocket gophers. They are stout and short bodied with dull-colored fur of gray, brown, sometimes almost black. They have inconspicuous, rounded ears, relatively small eyes, and short-to-medium tails.

Description, Habit, and Habitat

Voles are subterranean, living mostly below ground. However, they do spend considerable time foraging aboveground. Voles may be active day or night, and their activity patterns may change with the seasons. They do not hibernate and are therefore active and feeding all year. The young are born in nests below ground, and one female may have multiple litters in a year. They have a habit of using aboveground runways that are created from their movements and grazing. These runways are usually visible and easy to discover, one of the best field marks that voles are present.

Voles, like most other rodents, prefer a habitat that offers protective cover. Weedy gardens, abandoned fields, snow-covered fields, and fallow plots are ideal settings for meadow mice. Their preference for protective habitats makes winter gardens highly susceptible to feeding damage, since this is a time when most people aren't as diligent about weeding. Fruit trees are also at risk in areas where snow is plentiful. Hidden by the snow, voles take up residence in the root structure of the trees. Damage is not visible until the spring thaw, when it is often too late to save the trees.

Damage Characteristics

Most often, a gardener sees burrowing activity before seeing damage on a crop. Unlike pocket gophers, voles do not plug their tunnels with dirt. They keep their entrances open and often connect two or more entrances with a runway. Each burrow entrance is about 1½ to 2 inches in size, about the size of a golf ball. Often there are several entrances in a small area.

Voles are primarily vegetarians, feasting on grasses, forbs, tubers, bulbs, fruits, and nuts. Feeding damage occurs on all parts of the plant that are near or below ground level. On the West Coast, vegetable and bulb plants such as artichokes, brussels sprouts, beets, lilies, potatoes, horseradish, dichondra, and turf are susceptible. In the East and the Pacific Northwest, voles prefer fruit trees, particularly apple, causing the most damage in winter.

Another telltale sign of voles is the marks they leave on plants with their incisor teeth. On woody plants, check for very small grooves on the damaged part of the plant. These incisor marks can be difficult to see.

Management and Prevention Strategies

Voles generally don't scamper about the garden, so few people feel as kindly toward them as they do toward rabbits. Nevertheless, both nonlethal and lethal methods are available for controlling voles.

Exclusion   It is difficult to construct a fence that will keep voles out of a garden. Your best bet is to surround individual trees or plants with wire or nylon mesh. Protect raised beds by covering plants with conventional garden netting that has a mesh of 1 inch or less.

Protect small seedlings or saplings by placing over them an empty quart-sized milk container opened at both ends. Similar containers, such as tin cans and plastic soda bottles, can also be cut to fit over small plants.

Top: Often the surface runways of a vole are visible aboveground. These paths run from burrow to burrow. Bottom: The entrances to vole burrows are tiny, about 1½ to 2 inches in size. You may find many entrances in a relatively small area.

Trapping   Voles are easily trapped. Depending on your personal preference, both live traps and kill traps are effective. Set traps in the runways so that the animal can enter the trap from either direction. Bait traps with rolled oats mixed with peanut butter, cookies, apples, corn, or any small grain.

Top: Check for vole damage by looking for very small grooves on all parts of the plant that are near or below ground level.
Bottom: Set traps for voles in the surface runway, baiting with rolled oats mixed with cookies, peanut butter, apples, corn, or any small grain. Leave the trap in one location until no more voles are caught, then move it to another surface runway and repeat the process.

Because voles are most active in early morning and early evening, set traps by midafternoon. Check them the following morning. If you have captured a vole, reset the trap in the same location. Continue to trap in this location until no more voles are caught. Then relocate the traps 10 to 15 feet away in another surface runway. Continue this practice until you have covered the entire vole habitat. Relocate live voles to an empty field or meadow away from people. Dispose of dead voles as you would rats or mice.

Once all the voles have been caught, destroy the tunnel entrances and surface runways with a shovel or hoe to discourage voles dispersed from other burrows from taking residence. Though trapping requires more time and effort than baiting, it can minimize vole damage.

Baiting   This control strategy is effective if you are having problems over a wide area or are confronting a large number of voles. The key to successful baiting is fresh bait, since animals are not attracted to that which is wet, stale, moldy, or old.

Place about a teaspoon of toxic bait aboveground, in the runway (do not use the bait applicator for any other purpose). Voles will discover the bait during normal activity. If you are concerned about exposing nontarget species to toxic bait, place it in a bait station such as a small can. Prebaiting with small grain or cereal greatly improves your chances of success.

Repellents   Repellents are available for voles, the most common being thiram. Climate and environmental conditions play a big part in the effectiveness of all repellents. Follow the label directions for best results.

Habitat alterations   Stringent weed control and removal of the available habitat are key to managing voles and minimizing their damage. If weeds are allowed to proliferate, voles can take advantage of this protective vegetative cover to reproduce in great numbers in a very short time.

Another way to discourage voles is by introducing a cat with good hunting instincts. Some cats are adept at catching voles, and might help reduce a vole population. However, if you are suffering heavy vole damage, a cat will probably not be very effective.

Place bait for voles in the surface runway, above the ground. If you are worried about other animals eating the bait, place the bait in a small can.

Snakes in the Garden

Snakes are generally placed in one of two categories: poisonous and nonpoisonous. If you can identify nonpoisonous snakes in your garden, consider letting them stay. They are excellent predators and can reduce rodents in your garden.

If you can't tolerate snakes of any kind, the best solution is to remove any object that can provide thermal protection. Cold-blooded animals, snakes seek out woodpiles, overturned flower pots, heavy vegetation, and litter to protect themselves from heat or cold. The cleaner and neater you keep your garden area, the less attractive it is to snakes.

In the Southwest, snakes, particularly rattlesnakes, seek out patios at night to absorb the collected heat from the day. Little can be done to discourage this behavior. Fencing may help if you choose a woven mesh small enough to discourage the snake from passing through. An experimental rattle-snake trap has been designed, but it is not yet commercially available.

Aboveground Pests

The animal pests that live above the ground range in size from mice to deer.

Animal pests that live aboveground are usually active during the day, are not easily frightened by people, and are often observed by the gardener. Determining management strategies for these animals is often easier because you have a clearer window into their behavior than you do for below-ground pests.

If you are like many people, you probably view deer, hares, and tree squirrels as charming creatures. However, when these animals choose your garden as a feeding ground, their charm wears off rather quickly. Fortunately, you can use nonlethal means to reduce damage and still enjoy the wonders of these otherwise delightful animals.

Not many people are sympathetic to another group of aboveground pests—rats and mice. Often viewed with repulsion, these species cause considerable damage to gardens, attics, and homes, particularly in urban areas. Although most gardeners favor the lethal disposal of rats and mice, there are nonlethal methods for gardeners who wish to give these pests a second chance.

These graceful and charming creatures can be a gardener's nightmare.

DEER

Deer are adaptable animals, often found in areas many people would consider unlikely for such a large species. They can be serious garden pests even in residential areas where the house density is more than two houses per acre. Residential areas most attractive to deer have abundant food, water, shelter, and space, which are necessary to make suitable deer habitat. Deer often live out their entire lives in an area less than one square mile if the area has heavy ground canopies. They fancy many common ground plants including roses, fruit trees, shrubs, and even turf.

There are two species of deer found throughout North America, the mule deer (*Odocoileus hemionus*) and the white-tailed deer (*O. virginianus*).

The North American elk or wapiti (*Cervus elaphus*), the moose (*Alces alces*), and the caribou (*Rangifer tarandus*) are all taxonomically considered deer. These species are not usually viewed as garden pests. But if they sometimes cause problems in your yard, the suggestions in this chapter will apply to them as well.

Description, Habit, and Habitat

Deer, like sheep and cattle, are ruminants, or cud chewers. Their stomach is divided into four chambers—the rumen, the abomasum, the omasum, and the reticulatum. The bacteria and protozoa living inside the digestive system break down the celluloid fibers of plant cell walls. Deer chew, swallow, and rechew their food several times to maximize digestion of plant material.

Most ruminants must eat 3 percent of their body weight daily in order to sustain themselves. For example, a 1,000-pound cow must eat 30 pounds of grass a day to maintain its weight; a 250-pound sheep, 7.5 pounds of forage a day; and a 175-pound deer, about 5.25 pounds a day,

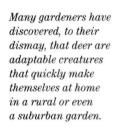

Many gardeners have discovered, to their dismay, that deer are adaptable creatures that quickly make themselves at home in a rural or even a suburban garden.

an amount of forage that would fill a large-sized garbage bag. Ruminants need a good deal of time to eat and digest that much forage.

Unlike cattle and sheep, which tend to be grazers, deer are browsers. They prefer a diet that has a high percentage of semiwoody material mixed with some forbs and they also forage on grass.

When feeding, deer are often mobile, not staying in one spot for very long. They are constantly searching for browse that is palatable and high in protein.

Damage Characteristics

Deer can cause immense amounts of damage in a garden. Once they find an attractive plant, such as a rosebush or apple tree, they will browse it heavily, often badly damaging it.

Most plants can tolerate a limited amount of browsing. However, browsing can greatly reduce the aesthetic appeal of garden landscaping. Deer often take the most accessible part of the plant, the newest growth. Large animals, they can browse at ground level up to a height of approximately 5 feet.

The most common type of damage deer cause is the removal of terminal and lateral buds. The removal of the terminal bud from a

Top: Although most gardeners will never be bothered by moose, the same methods that work for deer are effective with these extremely large pests. Bottom: Seedlings are often damaged by browsing. Deer can browse from ground level up to a height of approximately 5 feet.

woody, coniferous seedling forces the plant to grow in a shape resembling a bush rather than a tree. The tree is still biologically healthy, but its aesthetic appeal has been diminished.

Deer browsing can severely stunt the growth of newly planted fruit and nut trees, in some cases delaying their potential for fruit production by several years. These trees must be protected until they grow beyond the reach of deer.

Deer can also be pests in vegetable and flower gardens. They damage plants by stepping and trampling on them, and feed readily on small vegetable plants and herbs. An adult deer can remove an entire young lettuce plant in a single bite! Leafy vegetables, legumes, ground covers, and flowers are the garden plants most at risk.

A seasonal problem occurs in mid- to late summer when male deer rub their antlers on trees, fence posts, poles, and other rough surfaces to remove their shedding velvet. This activity is not a severe threat to older, established trees, but can devastate saplings.

Management and Prevention Strategies

Nearly all the options available for preventing damage caused by deer are nonlethal. Although deer-eaten rosebushes can certainly be maddening to gardeners, few want the deer to be killed—they just want the animals out of their gardens.

Portable electric fencing can be quickly erected to help keep deer out of your garden.

Habitat alterations   Cultural modification to reduce or eliminate suitable deer food and shelter in an area is rarely possible. Garden trees, vines, shrubs, small vegetables, and herbs other than grass are often highly preferred foods, especially during the growing season. Planting other forage or foliage as a trap crop (see page 22) to divert deer from valued garden plants may make the area more attractive to deer and worsen the problem.

Large-scale exclusion   The most effective long-term solution to minimizing deer damage is fencing. Although installing a fence is costly, the one-time expense pays for itself in short order. Whatever fence design you select, you need to check the structure periodically to ensure that it is functioning as intended.

A conventional deer fence can be constructed of any material that effectively excludes deer. It should have a minimum height of 8 feet. For gardens that approach a quarter acre in size, the best material is 4-inch woven wire (a smaller mesh size can be substituted if other, smaller pests such as rabbits, hares, or ground squirrels are also present). Ten-foot metal fence posts, also called T posts, should be buried 2 feet deep and spaced every 10 feet. The corner posts are constructed of 4×4 lumber in an H or double H design. The wire is secured to the ground with wire staples or buried a few inches into the soil.

Conventional Deer Fence

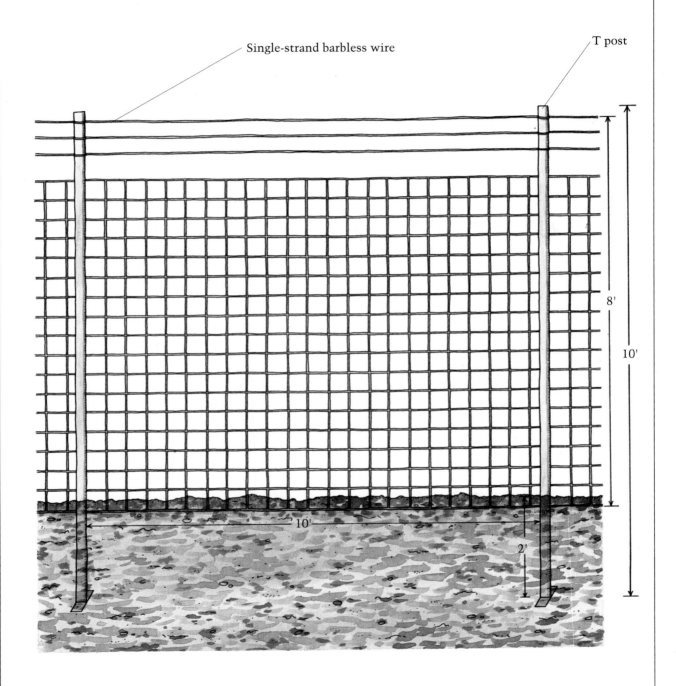

Single-strand barbless wire

T post

8'

10'

10'

2'

A conventional fence designed to keep out deer should reach a height of at least 8 feet. Woven wire is then secured to the posts, which are usually spaced 10 feet apart, and is either stapled to the ground or buried a few inches into the soil. Single-strand barbless wire is effective across the top of the fence.

Angled Deer Fencing

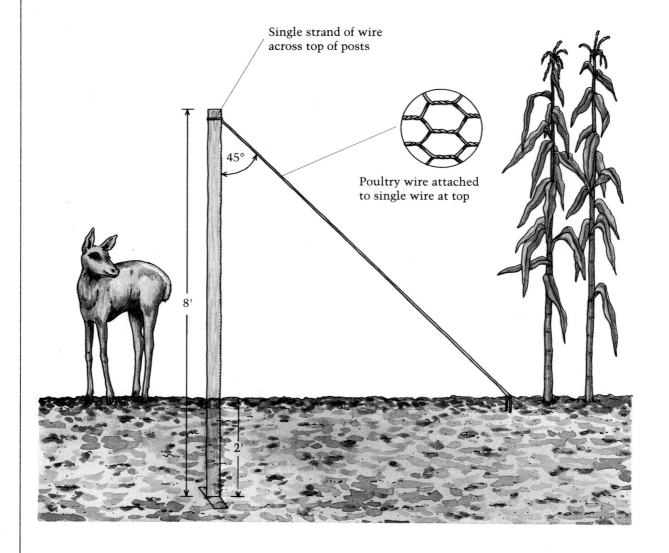

Single strand of wire across top of posts

Poultry wire attached to single wire at top

45°

8'

2'

If you want a fence that is not as high as a conventional deer fence, a slanted fence works well. The added spread of the fence and its angle creates the illusion of a fence that is too broad to jump over.

A slanted deer fence is similarly built but does not require the same height. Eight-foot T posts are used, spaced 10 feet apart and buried 2 feet deep. With this design the ½-inch poultry wire can be substituted for 4-inch woven wire used in conventional fencing. The poultry wire must be 8 feet high (this may require attaching two sections of 4-foot wire). A single strand of fencing wire is attached to the tops of the T posts to connect all the posts. The poultry wire is attached to this top wire, then the bottom is pulled at a 45-degree angle away from the posts toward the garden. The poultry wire is then attached to the ground with wire wickets, staples, or some other means.

You now have a fence that is 6 feet high, having a 45-degree angle. As the deer walks up to the fence, it comes under the overhang. This design creates an illusion of a fence that is too broad to jump over. The deer now must not only jump a 6-foot vertical fence, but it must also span a width excess of 10 feet. This very effective design is popular with the forest industry throughout the Pacific Northwest.

A less traditional approach is high-tensile electric fence. These fences are adapted from livestock fences used in Australia and New Zealand. They require far less material than conventional fencing and can be made with material that has a longer life span than the woven wire used to make conventional fences. The greatest savings with the high-tensile fence is the reduced need for fence posts. Depending on the terrain, a high-tensile fence requires a fence post only every 60 to 65 feet rather than every 10 feet as is the case with a conventional fence.

Although metal T posts can be used for the support posts, the corner posts must be made to withstand pressures of up to 250 pounds of pull from as many as nine wires. In this design the corner posts are usually 8-inch or 10-inch creosote-treated lodgepole pine. The poles must be a minimum of 10 feet in length. They are buried 4 feet deep with 6 feet aboveground. The pole is then notched, and a 4- or 6-inch brace post is anchored diagonally to the corner post of the fence. The brace is held in place by a breast block. The most common type of breast block is a 4-foot section of 4 × 4 or 6 × 6 lumber, although any other appropriate material, such as large stones or concrete blocks, can be used as an anchor. The breast block is buried approximately 12 inches into the soil. Once the brace is securely in place between the corner post and the breast block, the block can then be buried.

All these fence designs are applicable if you are interested in a perimeter fence surrounding your entire garden. They are meant to be permanent and cannot be easily disassembled or moved. In most cases these large-scale fences are recommended for gardens that are a minimum of one acre in size.

If you do not require permanent fencing, you may wish to consider portable electric fencing. Modern designs include poly-wire mesh fences that have a woven metal ribbing, for increased conductivity. They are lightweight and extremely versatile. They can easily be assembled to protect any part or all of your garden and then disassembled and stored when not needed. Take care to attach warnings to your electric fences.

All deer, including elk and moose, can severely damage fences. A well-maintained fence can be an effective deterrent. A poorly maintained fence can invite problems by entangling animals, allowing them to enter a garden but not to escape, or trapping them in your garden, thus endangering yourself and others.

Remember, no matter what fence design you choose, deer prefer to go under a fence rather than over it. You must ensure that the wire is securely fastened to the fence posts and that an animal cannot lift the fence to slip underneath.

Small-scale exclusion For many gardeners the word exclusion creates images of huge perimeter fences that are costly to construct and maintain. Exclusion of this kind is not always necessary. Deer may browse on only one plant, or you may wish to protect some plants and allow animals to feed on others. In these situations small exclusionary fences may be the solution.

For example, if deer are feeding on strawberry plants or other low-growing plants that are confined to beds, place sections of nylon garden netting over the top of the plants when deer are most likely to visit. If the plants or bushes are producing fruit, install corner posts to elevate the netting to any desired height. For strawberries, netting elevated 12 inches above the plants allows enough room for you to reach under and harvest the berries. If bush berries need protection, construct a frame to hang the netting to any desired height and secure it to the soil. This allows you to enter the protected area and harvest the fruit. You can remove these nets when they are no longer needed.

Constructing individual cages around plants is also a sound exclusion method. Drive two or more wooden or metal stakes into the ground. Then wrap 2-inch poultry wire or wire mesh around the stakes to form a circle around the plant, about 4 or 5 feet high. The diameter of the cage depends on the size of the plant. Leave these cages in place until the plant has grown beyond the reach of the deer. Fruit trees take several years to reach this height.

If the plant is small, use a nylon mesh bag as a protective barrier. You can obtain nylon mesh bags, which are used to ship produce, at your market. Drive two stakes into the ground near the plant and place the mesh bag over them to cover the plant. The mesh allows enough light and air to reach the plant. In the more humid areas of the country, check periodically for fungal or bacterial pathogens. Mesh bags may not be aesthetically acceptable in all situations. However, if the plant is a vigorous species like eucalyptus, you can remove the bag after one growing season.

Trunk protectors such as Vexar tubes can also protect small trees or vines. They're useful until the plant outgrows them. The tubes will eventually disintegrate, but they can be removed once their usefulness is finished.

Small-Scale Deer Exclusion

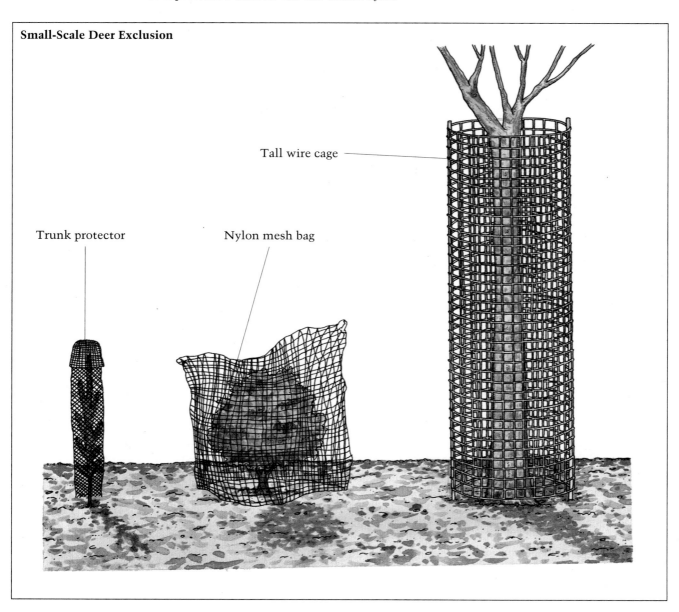

Trunk protector

Nylon mesh bag

Tall wire cage

Deer-Resistant Plants

The following plants have demonstrated some resistance to deer browsing, especially to the western species of deer. Ornamentals marked with an asterisk have been found to be unattractive to white-tailed deer (*O. virginianus*) in a study conducted in Connecticut. Other plants in the list may fall prey to white-tailed deer.

Abies fraseri* Fraser fir
Adolphia californica
Agapanthus africanus Lily-of-the-Nile
Agave americana Century plant
Aloe species Aloe
Aquilegia species Columbine
Aralia spinosa Hercules'-club
Arbutus unedo Strawberry tree
Artemisia tridentata Basin sagebrush
Arundo donax Giant reed
Bambusa* species Bamboo
Beaucarnea recurvata Elephantfoot tree
Betula pendula* Weeping birch
Buddleia davidii Butterfly bush
Buxus species Boxwood
Cactaceae species Cactus
Calendula officinalis Pot marigold
Calycanthus occidentalis Western spicebush
Casuarina stricta She oak
Chamaerops humilis European fan palm
Choisya ternata Mexican orange
Clematis species Clematis
Coprosma repens Mirror plant
Correa species Australian fuchsia
Cotinus coggygria Smoke tree
Cytisus scoparius Scotch broom
Daphne species Daphne
Datura species Thornapple
Delphinium species Larkspur
Digitalis species Foxglove
Diospyros virginiana Persimmon
Echinocystis lobata Wild cucumber
Echium fastuosum Pride-of-Madeira
Erythea armata Mexican blue palm
Fabiana imbricata Chile heath
Ferns
Ficus species Fig
Fraxinus velvutina Arizona ash
Gelsemium sempervirens Carolina jessamine
Hakea suaveolens Sweet hakea
Hedera canariensis Algerian ivy
Hedera helix English ivy
Helleborus species Hellebore
Hippophae rhamnoides Sea buckthorn
Hypericum species St. John's wort
Ilex species Holly (except thornless)
Iris species Iris
Jasminum species Jasmine
Juniperus species Juniper

Kerria Japonica Japanese rose
Kniphofia uvaria Devil's-poker, red-hot poker
Leptodactylon californicum Prickly phlox
Leucojum species Snowflake
Leucothoe fontanesiana Doghobble
Lonicera japonica Hall's honeysuckle
Lupinus species Lupine
Lyonothamnus floribundus Catalina ironwood
Magnolia species
Mahonia species
Melaleuca leucadendron Cajeput tree
Melia azedarach Chinaberry tree
Melianthus major Honeybush
Mesembryanthemum species Ice plant
Myrica californica Wax myrtle
Narcissus species Daffodil, narcissus
Nerium oleander Oleander
Nolina parryi Nolina
Oxalis oregana Redwood sorrel
Papaver species Poppy
Phoenix species Date palm
Phormium tenax New Zealand flax
Picea abies* Norway spruce
Picea glauca* White spruce
Picea pungens* Colorado blue spruce
Pinus mugo* Mountain pine
Pinus strobus* White pine
Pinus sylvestris* Scotch pine
Populus nigra italica* Lombardy poplar
Prunus caroliniana Carolina cherry laurel

Pueraria thunbergiana Kudzu vine
Pyrus communis* Pear
Quillaja saponaria Soapbark tree
Rhododendron species Rhododendron, except azalea varieties
Rhus ovata Sugarbush
Robinia pseudoacacia Black locust
Romneya coulteri Matilija poppy
Rosmarinus officinalis Rosemary
Rudbeckia hirta Black-eyed Susan, gloriosa daisy
Sabal blackburniana Hispaniolan palmetto
Sambucus racemosa Red elderberry
Schinus molle California pepper tree
Schinus polygamus Tree pepper
Solanum species Nightshade
Spartium junceum Spanish broom
Spiraea* species Bridalwreath
Syringa vulgaris* Common lilac
Syzygium paniculatum Eugenia
Tecomaria capenisis Cape honeysuckle
Teucrium fruticans Germander
Trachelospernum jasminoides* Star jasmine
Trachycarpus fortunei Windmill palm
Trillium species
Tulipa species Tulip
Viburnum tomentosum* Snowball viburnum
Washingtonia species Washingtonia palm
Zantedeschia species Calla lily
Zauschneria species California fuchsia
Zinnia species

An all too common sight for gardeners is a sea of decapitated flower stalks with their heads neatly snipped off by deer.

Repellents   A variety of chemical taste repellents are commercially available to prevent deer from browsing on trees, vines, and ornamental plants. In addition, gardeners have experimented for decades with household materials and other, more exotic, organic products to develop taste and odor repellents of their own. Materials have ranged from soap and human hair to lion dung.

When selecting a repellent, bear in mind that it must not be injurious to the plant. Also, do not apply commercial repellents to edible crops unless such use is specifically indicated on the product label.

Keep taste repellents on the plants at a high enough concentration to make the plants distasteful to deer. Exposure to excessive moisture in the form of sprinkler irrigation, humidity, and precipitation renders taste repellents ineffective. To maximize potency, apply these repellents before damage occurs and do so frequently to maintain suitable concentration levels. Also apply to new foliage as it develops.

One of the most common taste repellents is thiram, which was originally developed as a seed protectant. Other commercial taste repellents include those made of putrescent whole egg solids and an ammonium soap with higher fatty acids. These three products cause an unpleasant taste sensation when ingested. Be sure to follow the label directions carefully, since each product has strict guidelines on how to use it.

One home remedy that seems to have some merit is the mixture of ground cayenne pepper, cooking oil, and water. Many gardeners feel strongly that the pepper produces enough of a negative stimulus to repel deer. The cooking oil acts as a sticking agent for the pepper to adhere to the plant. A common formula is 1 tablespoon cooking oil, 4 or 5 tablespoons cayenne pepper, and 1 gallon water.

Before spraying an entire plant with this mixture, try it first on a small portion. If the leaves do not discolor or die within a few days, then spray the solution on the rest of the plant.

Odor repellents must be very pungent and concentrated. Gardeners have collected such materials as human hair from barbershops or lion and other predator dung from local zoos and spread them at the base of their plants. These materials repel deer only temporarily. Tests conducted in California have demonstrated that they do not reduce deer damage for extended periods.

Bar soap has long been promoted as a deer repellent. Gardeners have hung whole bars of soap or shavings in small cheesecloth bags from the branches of plants. A recent study conducted at a major university showed that

Many gardeners swear that a small cheese-cloth bag filled with soap or soap shavings helps repel deer from an area.

this method was approximately half as effective as commercially produced repellents. The study also demonstrated that the soap protects only small areas immediately surrounding it. In order for soap to reach the level of effectiveness of commercially produced repellents, the study showed, 450 bars of soap per acre would have to be applied.

Gardeners have also hung strips of cotton material soaked in concentrated bone tar oil from the plant. This method has proved somewhat effective.

Many gardeners reduce the browsing in their gardens by choosing plants that are not attractive to deer. The chart on page 63 lists plants that have been found to be resistant to the western species of deer, although many of the plants are not resistant to white-tailed deer. Your local agricultural office may have lists of plants that are deer-resistant in your area.

But when deer are hungry and the garden contains highly preferred foods, or when dense, severely competitive deer populations are present, repellents will most likely be ineffective.

Frightening devices In urban or residential areas, where deer often come into contact with humans, frightening devices are not often successful. Any noises deer encounter on a daily basis—lawn mowers, human voices, automobiles—become part of their routine. For a sound to be effective, it must present the threat of real harm. For example, the recording of a dog barking is not as effective as a real dog barking and chasing the animal. A radio playing loudly is not as effective as a real person shouting and chasing the animal, waving a rake!

A number of sonic devices are commercially available through retail outlets. However, tests conducted at the University of California at

Davis proved that these devices do not repel animals for very long. A deer becomes accustomed to the sound of any noisemaking device in a very short time. Once the animal discovers that the sound is harmless, it loses its fear of the noise.

Visual frightening devices such as scarecrows have some merit, but you must take the time to move the figure throughout the garden several times a week. If it remains stationary deer will come to view it as another permanent component of the landscape.

Shooting   In rural areas shooting is an effective option in reducing deer damage. It is not always necessary to kill all the deer that visit your garden. Sometimes the threat of danger is sufficient cause for the animals to seek forage in another location.

Deer are considered game species throughout North America. Therefore, they are under the jurisdiction of state or provincial governments. First obtain permission from local authorities. Even if you choose to shoot deer during regularly scheduled hunting seasons you need to purchase the necessary license and tags.

A word of caution. Many people hunt deer. An equal number of people enjoy watching them. Though hunters, deer watchers, and gardeners may agree that deer can cause substantial damage to a garden, few will agree that shooting deer is the proper solution. Even local game wardens are reluctant to issue depredation permits to kill damage-causing deer. For these and other reasons, consider shooting only after you have tried all other management options and failed.

Aversives   The timber industry in the Pacific Northwest tested an aversive a number of years ago. The aversive was selenium in tablet form, placed into the planting holes of Douglas fir seedlings. The selenium was designed to make the seedlings taste bad and condition the deer to avoid them. Unfortunately, the high concentration of selenium needed to repel deer also proved lethal to the trees.

Currently, there are no commercially available aversive products. However, the pepper-and-oil solution described on page 64 may condition deer to avoid specific plants if the solution is applied to them.

Habitat alterations   One of the most widely accepted control practices is the planting of deer-resistant plants. You can find the names of these plants on a number of lists. Not all lists are applicable to every situation and deer herd. The list on page 63 was compiled from university research, scientific publications, and several horticultural resources.

Jasmine is considered a deer-resistant plant.

HARES

Hares differ from rabbits in that they do not dig burrows and they rely on speed rather than agility to escape danger. Their young are born in a precocial state, able to move about, their eyes open. Hares are more apt to be seen in open fields and meadows. Their ability to outrun danger allows them to stray great distances from protective cover.

Hares resemble rabbits in outward appearance, though they have longer ears and feet and are generally larger than cottontails. Hares eat the same kinds of food as rabbits and are likewise active throughout the year. While they are active throughout the day, hares prefer to do most of their foraging during the night. They don't hibernate. They seek protection from the elements by constructing a simple nest, sometimes called a form, under a bush or tree.

Hares can jump but usually do so only when escaping danger. Like rabbits, hares can produce more than one litter per year and respond quickly to environmental factors that favor reproduction.

Description, Habit, and Habitat

In North America there are several species of hares. Those of greatest concern to the gardener include the black-tailed jackrabbit (*Lepus californicus*), the white-tailed jackrabbit (*L. townsendii*), and the snowshoe hare (*L. americanus*). These three species are responsible for the bulk of damage sustained in residential and rural areas. If you live in an area where one of the less common species occurs, you can still apply the methods given below.

Both the snowshoe hare and the white-tailed jackrabbit change the color of their fur

Hares, or jackrabbits, are attracted to many of the plants that attract rabbits. The methods for dealing with these two pests are often the same.

Jackrabbits do not burrow, so it is not necessary to bury a fence to keep them out. You may still wish to do this, however, if you are also bothered by ground squirrels, woodchucks, or other rodent species.

during the year. In summer the fur of both species is brown. With the onset of autumn they molt and change to a white winter coat. As spring nears they molt back to their summer brown color. This ability to change the color of their fur allows them to blend with their surroundings as the seasons change.

Damage Characteristics

Tender garden crops, the same ones that attract rabbits, often fall victim to hares. Small trees, shrubs, turf, and even some flowers may also be damaged. Their sharp incisors can clip off a branch at a crisp 45-degree angle. Damage can occur the year around. Tracks are easily distinguishable in the snow.

Management and Prevention Strategies

Many of the strategies used for cottontails can also be used for hares.

In many parts of North America, hares, particularly jackrabbits, can overpopulate. Rabbit plagues, as they are sometimes called, are cyclical and are a response to climatic and other environmental factors. If you are live in an area that is experiencing a population explosion of hares, contact local wildlife resource agencies.

Exclusion   When designing an exclusionary barrier for hares, follow the same procedure for excluding rabbits (see page 47). If both deer and hares are causing problems and you are considering construction of a wire fence, the fence mesh should not be greater than 3×3 inches. This mesh size will exclude deer, rabbits, and hares, providing it is installed at the height recommended to keep out deer.

Because hares will usually not burrow under a fence, it is not necessary to bury the fence into the soil. However, if ground squirrels, woodchucks, or other rodent species are also present, burying the lower portion of the fence will prove helpful overall.

Cages and similar structures around individual plants, seedlings, and saplings are very effective in providing long-term protection as is garden netting placed over strawberries, ground covers, and other low-growing plants.

Baiting   Several states allow the poisoning of jackrabbits. You must check with local agricultural authorities to determine which products are legally registered for home use in your state or region. Ask about restrictions on how and when poison bait is to be used and how to keep the bait away from nontargets such as children and pets. Some states permit only certified professionals to handle toxicants.

Shooting   If shooting is safe and legal in your area, the best time to shoot hares is at night when they are foraging. Once hares are alerted to your presence, however, it is difficult to kill more than one per night. Therefore, to achieve success, it may be necessary to spend several consecutive nights trying to shoot hares.

Using a firearm as a frightening device also has some merit as long as you live in an area where this is feasible. Shooting over the heads of the animals for several nights may frighten them into seeking forage elsewhere.

Repellents   Many of the repellents available for cottontails are also registered for jackrabbits. The procedures are also the same (see page 48). In addition, many deer repellents are applicable to hares (see page 64). Check labels to find the best product for your situation.

Habitat alterations   Hares, like rabbits, are often limited in the size of the food they can eat. Generally, stems, branches, and trunks larger than ¼ inch in diameter are too large for them to clip. If hares are a problem in your garden and you want to plant woody plants, select those that have limbs and branches larger than ¼ inch in diameter. This will not prevent hares from eating the bark and girdling the seedling, but it will discourage and prevent them from eating the entire plant.

TREE SQUIRRELS
Like deer and rabbits, tree squirrels are considered game animals. They are afforded special protection under game management laws of the various states and provinces. Consequently, there are limitations on minimizing tree squirrel damage.

Description, Habit, and Habitat
Tree squirrels are generally separated into three main groups. The first group, the fox and the gray squirrels, includes the species most commonly seen in city parks, suburbs, and wildlands. The second group, referred to as pine squirrels, includes the red squirrels and the Douglas squirrels found in forests. The third group, the flying squirrels, is the only nocturnal

The red fox squirrel, Scirus niger, is often found in city parks, suburbs, and wildlands throughout the country.

Tree squirrels will remove the bark of a redwood to feed on the sugary sweet layer just beneath, damaging the tree in the process.

species of tree squirrel and is rarely responsible for damaging gardens and homes.

All tree squirrels prefer acorns, beechnuts, hickory nuts, walnuts, pine nuts, almonds, corn, mushrooms, and soybeans. They are opportunists and can exploit any available food source. Fruit, buds, seeds, berries, cereals, insects, mushrooms, and woody plants are seasonal foods. Under normal conditions tree squirrels obtain water from the succulent forbs of their diet. During drought conditions they depend on freestanding water found in many gardens.

Tree squirrels are active during the day. They are easily distinguishable from ground squirrels and chipmunks by their larger size, bushy tails, and lack of spots or stripes over their body. Though their name implies that they live in trees, they spend extended periods of time foraging on the ground. Tree squirrels do not hibernate. They remain active throughout the year and rely on stored food caches to help them survive the cold winter months.

Damage Characteristics

Tree squirrels are responsible for damage to seeds, crops, trees, ornamentals, telephone cables and poles, and irrigation tubing. They even chew wooden buildings or invade attics through knotholes and other openings. Tree squirrels may carry a variety of diseases that are transmissible to humans.

In nut orchards and gardens, tree squirrels can severely curtail production by eating the nuts before harvest. In some parts of the East, gray squirrels eat the blossoms of cherry and pear trees.

In the Pacific Northwest, tree squirrels often girdle the tops of coastal redwoods, Douglas fir, and pines. They remove the bark to feed on the sugary sweet cambial layer just beneath the surface. The squirrels often take the bark off in distinctive long circular strips, giving the tree the appearance of a striped barber pole.

Management and Prevention Strategies

All tree squirrels are protected to some degree by state or local regulations. Check with local wildlife resource agencies before applying any lethal control methods to them.

Exclusion   Tree squirrels are difficult to exclude from a yard. Protect small individual trees by covering them with garden netting. For large trees, which are difficult to cover with netting, use a wide collar.

Encircle the tree with a collar made of a 2-foot-wide strip of sheet metal, Plexiglass, or similar pliable material. Position the collar about 6 feet from the ground and attach it to the tree with encircling wires connected by springs to allow for tree growth. The collar prevents squirrels from climbing into the tree.

If squirrels are using telephone wires to enter your garden, you can impede them by installing 2- or 3-foot sections of lightweight, 3-inch-diameter plastic pipe around the wire. You should first check with the local telephone company for approval. Slit the pipe lengthwise, spread it open, and place the pipe over the wire. Squirrels crossing this part of the telephone wire set the pipe spinning and tumble.

If squirrels are becoming a nuisance in a structure you need to determine whether they are gaining access through an adjacent tree. If so, trim the tree to prevent the squirrels from jumping onto the roof. Repair any openings squirrels have made with heavy gauge, ½-inch poultry wire.

Repellents   Repellents that work for tree squirrels include moth crystals (paradichlorobenzene), mothballs (naphthalene), methalnonyl ketone, and thiram. Before using any of these repellents, check the labels carefully and follow application directions precisely.

Thiram painted onto the stems and trunks of garden shrubs and trees may provide temporary protection from chewing. Mothballs placed at the base of trees and shrubs may inhibit squirrels from climbing into their canopies. However, the effectiveness of these materials in the outdoors is questionable.

If squirrels are a problem in attics and buildings, mothballs may temporarily discourage them and cause them to leave. Seal the opening that allowed them access. Supplement this approach by leaving lights on or playing loud music.

Trapping   Tree squirrels can be trapped with a live trap size 1 or 2, and relocated to another site. Baits that attract squirrels include orange slices, apples, walnuts, peanut butter, and sunflower seeds. Place the traps in areas squirrels frequent most. Since the squirrels are active during the day, it is best to set the traps in the evening or early morning before they become active. Because of their status as game animals

you need to check local regulations before setting traps. Some states have strict guidelines about relocating wild animals.

Nuisance squirrels can be trapped and killed with a rat snap trap. Select a tree that squirrels often use and either place the traps at the base of the tree or secure the traps to a tree limb or branch with wire or twine. Be careful not to place the trap where it might attract birds. Nut meats placed on the trap treadle are an attractive bait.

Prebaiting increases your chances of catching the animals with either trapping method. Place the bait in the area of the tree where you expect to place the trap. Keep the location baited for 24 to 36 hours before installing the trap or until you have conditioned squirrels to regard the tree as an easy food source. Once they have been conditioned, replace the prebait with the trap, using the same bait.

In addition to damaging fruit and nut production, tree squirrels can also harm trees by girdling the trunk.

Traps for squirrels can be either live, as shown here, or lethal. Check local regulations before setting any traps.

Set the trap only during the day when squirrels are active so that nontarget animals are not caught during the night. Keep the traps set until you have removed all the squirrels. One trap can eliminate several squirrels in a short period of time. Remember that squirrels are a regulated game animal; check with local authorities before setting traps.

Baiting For most homeowners, there are no toxic baits available to eliminate tree squirrels. Five-percent zinc phosphide tracking powder, a restricted-use pesticide for houses and industrial and agricultural settings, can be applied only by a licensed pest control operator.

RATS AND MICE

No other group of small mammals elicits such a strong, negative response from humans as do rats and mice. Generally, the native species of North American rats and mice are not as much of a garden pest as the introduced European species. Native species are more often found in rural settings where human populations are relatively low.

Native Species

Native mice are generally referred to as deer mice or white-footed mice. Both names refer to the same group of woodland mice. The proper taxonomic name for the group is *Peromyscus.* These mice have thick fur of various color ranging from brown to almost black on top and white below. They have large ears and long, furred tails that are often bicolored, dark above and light below. Although these mice can invade homes and gardens in wooded or rural areas, they are not considered major garden pests.

North America has several species of native rats. The most attractive and biologically interesting are the wood rats, of the genus *Neotoma*, commonly referred to as pack rats. These rats collect objects and return to their nests to "pack" away their treasures, hence their name. Like deer mice, wood rats are common in wild forests, deserts, and woodlands, and are not often a problem in the garden or home.

Other species of native rats found in North America include cotton rats (*Sigmodon*) and kangaroo rats (*Dipodomys*). Neither is considered a major garden pest. However, if you suspect that a native species of mice or rats is causing problems, the solutions presented below for old-world species will prove effective.

Old-World Species

The introduced species of rats and mice, collectively referred to as old-world species, are taxonomically placed in the family *Muridae.* Rats are members of the genus *Rattus* and the house

Top: The roof rat, found in the West Coast, the Gulf states, and the Southeast, has become a considerable pest in suburban areas. Bottom: Deer mice (Peromyscus species) are native to North America and not as destructive to gardens and homes.

Cats are natural predators of rats and mice.

mouse belongs to the genus *Mus musculus.* Together they have been responsible for immense human suffering and have caused thousands of human deaths worldwide. Both can transmit such diseases as bubonic plague, leptospirosis, salmonella, murine typhus fever, and lymphocytic choriomeningitis. Their presence results in uncounted losses in cereal products, fresh fruit and nuts, livestock feeds, and other major foodstuffs. They are responsible for millions of dollars' worth of damage to structures and homes. Their bites produce bacterial infections and disfiguring scars.

The two species of rats found in North America are the Norway or sewer rat (*R. norvegicus*) and the black or roof rat (*R. rattus*). The Norway rat is the more widely distributed of the two species, found wherever humans are. This rat lives in a wide variety of settings and habitats, including cities, stream banks, garbage dumps, grain and cereal fields, and other locations where supplies of food, water, and cover are plentiful. The Norway rat is found throughout the contiguous 48 states, and in parts of Canada and Alaska.

The roof rat is confined to the West Coast, the Gulf states, and the Southeast. It is more often found in suburban areas with manicured gardens and lawns. It takes readily to backyards, attics, and storage sheds and can coexist with humans in most settings.

Description, Habit, and Habitat

The Norway rat is the larger of the two rats. A short, stocky rodent, an adult rat can weigh as much as a pound. The fur is short, shiny, and brownish in color. Its tail is not furred and is approximately as long as the combined length of its head and body. Its eyes and ears are relatively small for its body size. It is a good swimmer but not a good climber. In urban areas, Norway rats usually occupy the lower floors in multistoried buildings.

The roof rat is smaller and more slender than the Norway rat. Its tail is usually longer than the combined length of its head and body. Its eyes and ears are larger than those of the Norway rat and appear to be in better proportion to its overall body size. Fur color ranges from light tan to black.

Roof rats are excellent climbers and are often found living in trees and vine-covered patios and fences. They are also found in well-manicured gardens where food, cover, and water are plentiful. This species defies the conventional belief that rats live near litter, garbage, or other refuse.

The house mouse is a small, agile rodent. It is a slender animal that weighs from ½ to 1 ounce. It resembles a miniature model of the roof rat in color and appearance.

Although they prefer cereal grains, house mice consume a variety of foods. They have keen senses and are excellent climbers. House mice can enter a structure through a hole that is as small as ¼ inch wide. Once indoors they prefer to nest in hidden locations such as drawers, closets, boxes, crates, and walls. They are generally active at night, although they can be seen during the day.

Damage Characteristics

Rats and mice can damage fruit, flowers, trees, shrubs, and turf. They also gnaw on electrical wire insulation and water delivery systems. Their urine and droppings spoil food products and stain walls and ceilings. Their burrowing can weaken structural foundations, levees, concrete slabs, and raised garden beds.

The following signs indicate rodents are present in your garden or home.

• Droppings are deposited in runways, along shelves, behind refrigerators, or in areas where rodents are feeding. Droppings are large for rats (¾ inch in length and ¼ inch in diameter) and smaller for mice (about ¼ inch in length). They are often found in mass quantities. When fresh, the droppings have a soft texture. With prolonged exposure to air they darken and dry.

• Urine is visible when it is both wet and dry. When dry, urine appears as a whitish or

Outwitting Raccoons

These masked creatures are the most dexterous of garden pests, able to pry the lid off trash cans, open the latch of a garden gate, spring traps, and climb easily. Gardeners throughout the United States and southern Canada have tried hard to outwit raccoons.

Raccoons eat a varied diet, including insects, eggs, and mice as well as your garden plants. They tend to catch food near the water and play with it there before eating. Favorite foods include sweet corn and melons, and they will tear up sod to look for grubs. Their timing seems to be impeccable—they always strike just when the crop is at its peak. Their activity level tapers off in winter, but they never enter true hibernation, so you may encounter them the year around.

Repellents seem to work very well for raccoons. Leaving human-scented clothes or dog droppings in a garden often deters these nighttime visitors. Another remedy may be dusting crops with baby powder or ground hot peppers.

Fencing may be the best defense. Build a raccoon-proof fence of poultry wire that is at least 4 feet high. Bend the top 12 to 18 inches away from the garden. Be sure there are no tree branches or other ways for the raccoon to enter the garden over the fence. If you don't want to fence the entire yard, drape plants with bird netting or surround the entire garden with wire mesh. As a last resort, use a live trap to capture the animal and then relocate it. Check with local wildlife resource agencies for any restrictions or regulations. Since raccoons are mean when captured, you may wish to hire a professional to do this job.

yellowish stain. Stains are found in travel ways and feeding areas.

• Tracks include footprints and tail marks and are most often seen in dusty or muddy areas. If rats are using a travel lane, the dirt they leave from their feet becomes visible. Look for these travel lanes along walls, doorways, or some other vertical structure that provides cover. You can make a tracking patch in a suspected rat travel lane by placing ordinary baking flour in an area overnight and observing it the next morning for signs of activity.

• Travel lanes and burrows are obvious signs that you should look next to walls, foundations, and raised garden beds, and under bushes and debris. Rodents memorize the location and direction of their travel lanes and use them often.

• Rub marks are left by rats when they rub off body oil and dirt against walls, beams, rafters, and pipes. Repeated contact results in a darkened smudge.

• Gnawing is visible on doors, walls, garden hoses, storage containers, planter boxes, or any other surface where rodents are present. You should be aware of shavings, litter, or debris caused by their chewing.

Sounds such as scratching, chewing, climbing in the walls, squeaks, and fighting noises are common if rats are present.

Bait snap traps for rats and mice with cheese, bacon, peanut butter, or cake and cookie crumbs. Be careful to set them where non-problem animals won't encounter them.

Management and Prevention Strategies

The key to permanent damage reduction is a combination of population control and stringent sanitation practices that alter available habitat. Homeowners can probably control a few mice or rats successfully, but a significant population requires the help of a professional pest control operator.

Habitat alterations   The intended goal of good sanitation practices is to reduce food, water, and shelter. This ensures that rodent populations will not reestablish themselves in your home or garden after taking action to reduce them. Unfortunately, bird feeders and vegetable gardens provide food for these rodents, while plantings, woodpiles, and storage sheds provide safe harborage. It is unlikely that you will want to remove these items from your yard.

Effective sanitation practices include the following.

• Removal of pet foods when not in use and storage of pet foods and birdseed in rat-proof metal containers

• Proper disposal of refuse and garbage, including the omission of food items (vegetable tops, table scraps, animal food, and so on) in compost piles

• Weed control around buildings, gardens, and shops

• Firewood storage in neatly stacked piles 16 inches off the ground and with minimum space between wood

• Storage of planter boxes, containers, tools, and other garden materials in a manner that minimizes harborage

Exclusion   Seal all openings larger than ½ inch wide for rats and ¼ inch wide for mice to keep them from invading any structure. Fill the opening with steel wool, then cover it with hardware cloth or metal or aluminum sheeting. Do not use a chewable material, such as plastic or wood, to cover the opening.

Frightening devices   Studies conducted at the University of California at Davis on commercial ultrasonic devices have proved that many devices are ineffective in repelling rodents.

Baiting   A number of toxicants are registered for homeowner use against rats and mice.

When placing bait, you must take extra care to prevent consumption by children and nontarget animals such as pets and birds. The loss of a treasured family dog is far more painful than the presence of a couple of mice.

Always be sure to use fresh bait. Bait that is old, wet, stale, or moldy won't attract rodents.

Trapping Traps are very effective in eliminating individual rodents in gardens, homes, or sheds. They are somewhat limited in their effectiveness if you are dealing with a large population, which requires the help of a professional pest control operator. Set several traps simultaneously to achieve significant population reduction. Bait traps with cheese, bacon, peanut butter, or cake and cookie crumbs.

Snap traps can be placed behind structures and appliances and in doorways, bushes, and runways frequented by rodents. If rats are damaging fruit in trees or nesting in them, attach snap traps to a limb or trunk of the tree with wire. However, snap traps set in trees can also capture and kill other animals such as birds, chipmunks, and squirrels.

Glue boards are placed behind doors, along walls, or in any location rodents frequent. They are nontoxic and capture the rodents with a very sticky glue when they walk over it. The animals must then be killed and disposed of. It is inhumane to wait for the animal caught in these traps to die, as it will take days. If you use these traps, you must plan on killing the captured rodent. Their effectiveness is limited to mice.

If you set live traps to catch rats and mice, you need to decide what to do with them after you've caught them.

Natural predators Household pets, especially cats but also some dogs, often hunt mice and rats. Some other animals you might find to be garden pest control allies are snakes, hawks, and owls.

If you're lucky enough to have owls living nearby, you may soon discover how good they are at helping to eliminate many garden pests.

Fliers

Winged creatures can be both beneficial to the garden and a menace to crops.

Some of our most interesting wildlife species are those that fly. Birds of all shapes and sizes are often welcomed visitors to our gardens. Bats, another flier, are a common sight on warm, sultry summer nights as they flutter overhead in search of insects to eat.

Both birds and bats benefit our yards and gardens, consuming insects and pollinating fruit and nut trees. But they can also become pests. Learning to control the damage they do will help you enjoy their presence in your garden.

Birds are delightful wildlife visitors, if you can eliminate the damage they do to crops.

BIRDS

Birds can be divided into two major groups, residents and migrants. Resident birds are those individuals and species that stay in a particular area throughout the year. Sparrows, woodpeckers, crows, jays, starlings, grackles, and pigeons are among those birds that do not migrate between summer and winter home ranges.

Migrant species are those birds that travel considerable distances between summer and winter ranges to search for food and to avoid inclement weather. Migratory species include most waterfowl and wading birds, swallows, robins, hummingbirds, warblers, and hawks.

Resident and Migrant Birds

Recognizing that birds are either residents or migrants makes you aware of the seasonality of potential damage. Migratory species often congregate in large numbers in winter or summer areas and can cause severe economic damage in short periods of time. For example, migratory waterfowl by the tens of thousands often descend on grain and cereal crops in early autumn and consume the crops in a matter of hours. The same can happen in a garden when hungry birds concentrate during winter. A common seasonal problem occurs when sparrows and finches, which are nonmigratory, are attracted to garden bird feeders. The birds often remove the buds from fruit trees they're using as perches while waiting for their turn at the feeder.

Resident and migratory species can be found together seasonally when the migrants move into the resident's territory. This overlap often happens during fall and spring migrations. For instance, along most of the Pacific Coast, sparrows and finches are found in backyard gardens throughout the year. During winter and early spring, robins migrate to the coast to escape the extreme cold inland. Robins often stay along the coast long enough to feed on the first strawberries and bush berries in early spring. The resident sparrows and finches are usually not a problem for these early crops, but the seasonal robins often decimate them. This is just one example of how a seasonal migrant causes problems when the resident species have no negative impacts on the garden.

Resident birds such as crows, starlings, blackbirds, or grackles may congregate in a particular tree in early evening and spend the night there. Birds sometimes roost in the same tree night after night, year after year. Evidence suggests that crows in the Sacramento Valley of California have used the same roosts for decades. A particular roost may have as many as 1,500 birds per night. As humans encroach

Robins are migratory birds that may inflict seasonal damage on a garden crop.

into rural areas, bird roosts have become a nuisance to neighborhood residents. The large concentration of birds causes both an aesthetic problem from the noise they create and a public health problem from the massive amounts of manure they produce.

Birds often seem to have the uncanny ability to start feeding on ripening fruit the day before you plan to pick it. These birds probably spent the summer in your garden feeding on insects or seeds, waiting, like you, for the fruit to ripen. Recognizing the predictability of a seasonal problem such as this allows you to take appropriate steps to prevent damage or loss of fruit.

Before beginning a management program to control birds, you must first determine which bird species or groups of species are causing the problem. You need to be able to distinguish a robin from a woodpecker, a sparrow from a

starling, a hawk from a lark. The time of the year the damage is occurring can provide a clue as to whether the culprit is a seasonal or resident bird. Sometimes identifying individual species is not as important as identifying the group of birds. For example, if you have determined that blackbirds are the culprit, it will not be necessary to identify which species of blackbird is causing the problem (there are several species in North America).

Benefits and Problems of Attracting Birds

Many gardeners place bird feeders in their garden to attract birds. Birdseed, suet balls, orange slices, and nectar feeders are all effective in attracting birds. Many gardeners even plant seed-producing flowers and maintain hedgerows to attract birds. Although attracting birds can en-

Roosting blackbirds call these neighborhood power lines their nighttime home.

Resident birds, such as the yellow-headed blackbird (top) and the red-winged blackbird (bottom right), remain in one territory throughout the year. Finches (bottom left) are also often found in the garden the year around along the Pacific Coast.

hance your enjoyment of gardening, keep in mind that you may also be inviting trouble.

When designing your garden you should try to plan for birds to be an integral part of the landscape. Good planning will help you avoid problems that may occur later on. For example, if you choose to place a birdseed feeder in your garden, you should understand that you will attract seed-eating species. Therefore, do not place the feeder directly in or near an area of your garden where you plan to harvest seeds for future plantings (onions, carrots, marigolds, asters, sunflowers, and daisies, for example). Seed-eating birds do not distinguish between the seeds in the feeder and the seeds growing on the plant.

Another frustrating experience for gardeners is that seed-eating birds themselves may attract predators. Nearly everyone knows that cats discover bird feeder locations, and patiently wait for hours to pounce on seed-eating birds. In much of the country, there are laws against free-roaming cats, and you can legally trap them live and turn them over to your local animal shelter if they don't belong to a neighbor.

A more surprising predator is another bird. Many gardeners are taken aback when they witness a sharp-shinned hawk catch and kill a bird that they have purposely attracted to their garden. This is normal behavior and can be avoided only by excluding all birds from your yard, a highly unlikely circumstance. Birds attacking other birds may be a seasonal problem; sharp-shinned hawks, for example, vary their range to follow the movements of their prey birds.

Damage Characteristics

Most gardeners usually discover the damage caused by birds and other wildlife after the fact during routine garden maintenance. Bird damage is generally caused either by feeding on plant parts or by large numbers of birds congregating and depositing manure and damaging limbs and buds. It takes a trained eye to determine whether birds and not squirrels or other animals are injuring fruit, bark, or limbs.

Damage to seeds Many birds use seeds as a substantial part of their diets. Some, like quail, eat the leafy vegetable parts of a plant in win-

Strategically located bird feeders help keep seed-eating birds away from your plants.

Linnets have damaged this peach, picking at it as it ripened.

Keeping Opossums Out of the Garden

The opossum, the only native North American marsupial, is often considered one of the most unattractive animals to enter a garden. The size of an average cat, these animals have dirty gray fur, a white head that ends in a point, and a long tail. Its paws resemble tiny hands. They are found east of the Rocky Mountains and on the West Coast, usually near streams or swamps.

Opossums eat almost anything. Holes in compost piles, damaged and stripped tomato plants, bent cornstalks, and overturned trash cans may all be signs of these nocturnal raiders.

The best deterrent to these pests is keeping the garden clean. In particular, keep trash picked up and trash cans tightly sealed. Opossums can be excluded from the garden by a fence built of poultry wire that is at least 4 feet high, with the top 12 to 18 inches of fencing bent outward away from the garden and not attached to any support.

Live traps also work well for catching opossums. Bait the trap with bread and jelly, which won't attract cats. Check with local wildlife resource agencies for any regulations on trapping and releasing opossums.

Top: These cherries have been draped with nets to prevent birds from getting at the fruit.
Bottom: Strawberries are another favorite food of birds.

ter and spring but change their diets in summer and fall to feed almost exclusively on seeds. Others, particularly sparrows, finches, grosbeaks, and buntings, rely on seeds throughout the year to supply their nutritional needs. Take care to protect newly planted garden vegetable and flower seeds from crowned sparrows, finches, goldfinches, and juncos. These species are readily attracted to newly planted lawns and other plantings of small seeds. Larger seeds such as corn, sunflower, and cereal grain attract jays, crows, quail, and grosbeaks.

Damage to seedlings and vegetables Blackbirds, grackles, crowned sparrows, horned larks, house sparrows, and starlings often pull seedlings and young plants out of the ground and ingest the entire plant. Winter vegetables such as cauliflower and broccoli are very vulnerable to large winter flocks and can easily be destroyed.

Damage to fruits and nuts Birds enjoy eating ripening fruits and nuts. A bird can remove fruits and nuts in a single bite if they are small. The best evidence of bird damage to fruits and nuts that grow in bunches, such as grapes, pis-

tachios, and sometimes cherries, is when the bunches appear to have been "picked" at random. Birds often remove a single berry or nut, then retreat to a safe roost to eat it. After finishing, birds return to the same plant but not necessarily to the same bunch. After several trips, birds will have removed fruit from several bunches, giving them the appearance of having been partially picked or harvested. Finches,

The wounds caused by woodpeckers are unsightly, but seldom inflict serious damage to a tree.

jays, grackles, and sometimes robins (on bush berries) damage garden crops this way.

Robins, finches, jays, crows, magpies, and starlings go after larger fruits, such as strawberries, cherries, nectarines, peaches, and figs, eating only one side of the fruit.

Damage to limbs, branches, and trunks
Many gardeners confuse bird damage to the woody parts of a tree with insect damage caused by boring beetles or moths. Large holes can be caused by woodpeckers searching for food or using the trees as "drumming" perches when searching for a mate. Though the holes appear ominous, they seldom pose any real threat to the health of the tree.

The woodpecker species most often associated with drilling holes into fruit and nut trees is the sapsucker. When they feed, these birds drill large holes, in a continuous line, around the large branches or limbs of a tree and some-

times even around the main trunk. They then leave the limb for several days to allow sap to ooze from the wounds. Upon their return they feed on the sugary substance and on any insects that have been attracted to it.

The wounds that these birds inflict on trees are usually superficial and do not pose any serious threat. There are several old, abandoned apple orchards in the Pacific Northwest where the trees are still producing large quantities of fruit and thriving after decades of drilling by sapsuckers. The damage rarely penetrated deep in the cambial tissue. The trees usually repaired the wound with callus tissue and resumed normal function.

Damage to buildings and other structures
Woodpeckers can do substantial damage to buildings and other structures when caching food or attracting mates. They drill holes into siding and shingles and under the eaves of

buildings to search for insects or to excavate nest chambers. They can damage fence posts, telephone poles, and storage facilities. Drumming on buildings during the breeding season, they create vexing noise and further damage.

Pigeons, starlings, house sparrows, and swallows all coexist with humans, causing damage to buildings from their nesting or roosting activities and the manure they create.

Management and Prevention Strategies

Birds are protected by laws that specify what you can and cannot do to minimize damage. Most bird species that cause garden problems are legally classified as migratory nongame birds. You must obtain a permit before taking any bird species. However, permits are generally not required to scare or exclude depredating birds. Introduced species such as starlings, house sparrows, and pigeons may be controlled without a permit.

There are a number of strategies you can adopt to minimize bird damage in the garden. Usually, a combination of strategies is the most effective.

Exclusion Exclusion is a positive, long-term management approach. It is also perhaps the most practical. You can place lightweight plastic netting over seedbeds, vines, berries, and small trees. How you suspend the netting de-

Top: Netting is one of the simplest methods of keeping birds away from ripening fruits or vegetables. Bottom: Screens are also effective in keeping birds from damaging plants.

pends on the crop or plant. Strawberries and bush berries, for example, are relatively easy to protect with netting. Simply drape the material directly over the plants, or construct a frame or trellis to hold the netting over the plants so that it will not interfere with plant growth. Cover fruit from the time it begins to ripen until after harvest. Then remove the netting and store it for use the following year.

It may be somewhat more difficult to place netting over large trees, though this approach is still effective. Large-scale protection may be necessary to prevent bird damage to cherries, apricots, and grapes. Take extra care to ensure that the netting fits close to the ground around the trees. If you leave gaps or openings, birds can get under the netting and harm the plant or become entangled and harm themselves.

Cover row crops and other vegetables by constructing small frames made of plastic pipe, wood, or angle irons and cover with poultry wire mesh. Keep the mesh (½ inch is sufficient for birds) above the plants to minimize damage to growing plants and to permit weeding and harvesting.

Frightening devices　Gardeners have long devised a number of methods to scare birds. These have ranged from the traditional scarecrow to modern electronic devices. You must also remember that the effectiveness of all frightening devices diminishes greatly as the birds become accustomed to them.

Visual frightening methods such as scarecrows, flashing pie tins, moving shapes, artificial owls and snakes, flashing lights, and kites made to resemble a hovering hawk may provide temporary relief. Also popular are commercially available balloons that, when inflated, resemble large eyes. These, too, tend to keep birds at bay. But as time passes birds will not feel threatened by these inanimate objects.

Auditory frightening methods such as exploding booms, high-pitched sounds, and electronic noises are effective in agricultural settings, but are loud and disturbing to people in residential areas. For this reason, auditory methods are generally not recommended for gardens.

Studies conducted at the University of California demonstrate that using electronic recordings of crow distress calls can effectively chase birds from night roosts. A similar approach has been used with limited success on gulls at airports. Distress calls use the birds' own alarm signals to warn others of impending danger. The birds are less apt to become conditioned to the presence of such calls, so their effectiveness does not diminish as quickly. Distress call tapes are commercially available from Johnny Stewart Game Calls, generally marketed through outdoor outfitters. Currently, distress calls have very limited application, but ongoing research suggests this will improve.

Baiting　There are many legal restrictions on the use of toxic baits to control bird damage. Training is required to handle baits.

Repellents　Bird repellents are generally designed to discourage birds from landing, nesting, or roosting on the ledges of buildings. Chemical repellents are dispensed as a caulking on window ledges or structural gambrels. Plastic or nylon structures, resembling long, intertwined barbed wire that can repel birds from similar settings are commercially available. Follow directions on packaging for installation.

Commercial bird repellents that can be applied directly to crops do not exist for gardens. Many gardeners have experienced limited success spraying a mixture of cayenne pepper, water, and cooking oil on fruit crops (see page

Commercially available frightening devices may prove effective against birds, but relief is likely to be short term.

64). Wet conditions will limit the effectiveness of any repellent applied directly to the plant, and the repellent may damage the plant itself.

Shooting Shooting may work if the number of birds is small. Remember, only house sparrows, starlings, and pigeons (rock doves) are not protected species. They can be taken at any time.

You need a valid hunting license if you decide to shoot game species such as quail, doves, waterfowl, and pheasants. Find out when the hunting season begins and ends, bag limits, and the laws on firing guns near dwellings, roads, or other human habitats. Shooting birds is not an option for most people.

Habitat alterations Changes to the garden may make it less desirable to birds. Since many species of birds feed on seeds, reducing the number of seed-producing weeds also reduces

Top: Some bird repellents are dispensed as caulking along ledges to prevent birds from nesting.
Bottom: Birds are attracted to brush piles, brambles, and thickets. Eliminating or pruning these areas will help reduce the number of damage-causing birds in your garden.

the number of birds coming to forage in your garden. If weeds are allowed to grow unchecked, birds will establish a feeding ground and return to it frequently. Birds may stay and turn to crop seeds, seedlings, or fruits and vegetables when they become available.

Brush piles, brambles, and thickets all serve as hiding places for some birds. These protective areas allow birds to remain in the garden for extended periods of time. Prune or eliminate this vegetative cover to reduce harborage for birds.

By watching the birds that frequent your garden you should be able to identify the habitat characteristics that attract them and then modify or eliminate them accordingly.

Bats may be physically unattractive, but they are generally useful visitors to the garden, feeding on insects that damage plants.

BATS

Bats generally do not cause problems to garden plants. Indeed, many of them feed on insects during their nightly flights. Some gardeners even use commercially produced bat houses to attract these animals to their gardens. However, you should be aware that setting up a bat house does not guarantee it will be inhabited by a bat. These houses also attract wasps.

It is when bats invade homes that problems are caused. Bats that have taken up residence in a home produce foul odors and unsightly stains to ceilings and walls. Their presence can also unnerve any individual who wakes up in the middle of the night and sees a bat fluttering about the bedroom.

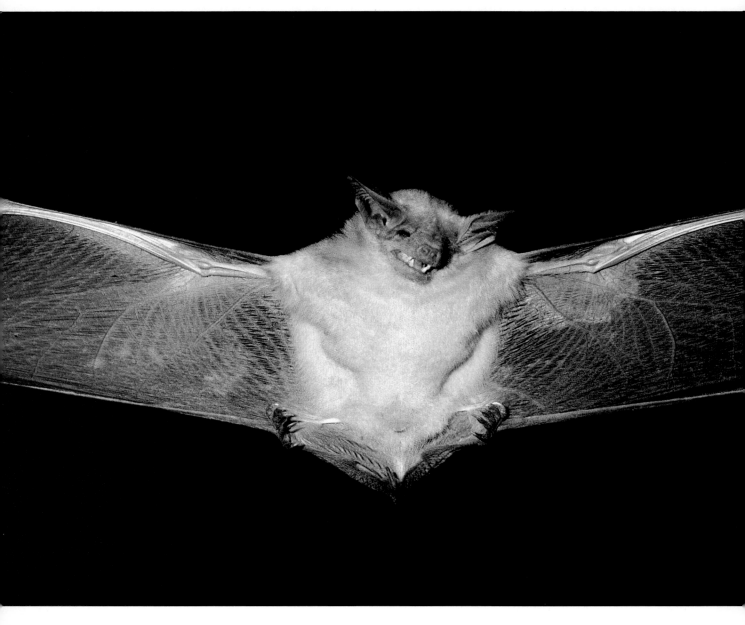

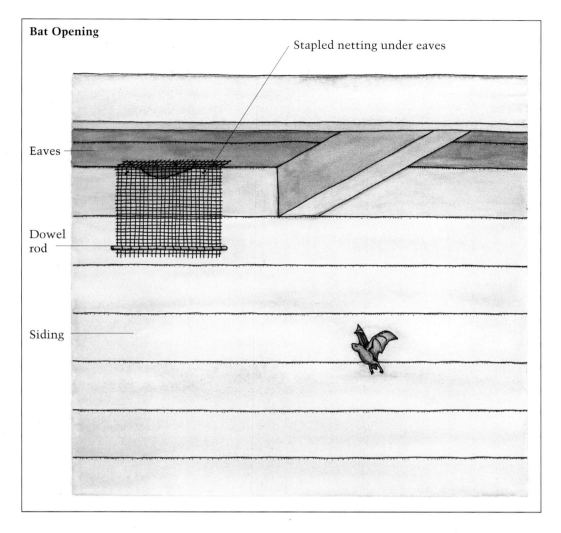

Bat Opening

Stapled netting under eaves

Eaves

Dowel rod

Siding

Bats are found under shingles and tiles of a roof, inside attics and walls, and in old outbuildings. Bats are frail animals and cannot move obstacles in their path. Therefore, they rely on already existing openings to enter and exit a structure.

Exclusion This is the only method that will eliminate bats from a house. Drive the animals from the building and then seal the opening to keep them from returning, or wait until they have flown out for the night and then seal the opening. Unfortunately, this means you will need to do all the repair work late at night, and it also presents the possibility of sealing a bat inside your home if not all have left.

A university researcher has introduced a relatively new approach to bat exclusion. He found that by designing a one-way, floppy door, similar to a pet door, bats could exit a structure but could not reenter it. The key to the researcher's approach is to eliminate all but one of the openings the bats are using. The bats will then be forced to use the remaining openings as the only entrance and exit.

Suspend a piece of nylon garden netting with ¼-inch mesh, or smaller, on the exterior side large enough to cover the opening. Tack the netting along the top margin only. You have now created a "drape" over the opening. To keep the netting from blowing in the wind attach fishing weights, wooden dowels, or similar objects to the bottom of the drape.

As the bats exit the building they fly into the drape and fall or crawl around the obstacle. Upon their return they again fly into the drape but are unable to negotiate the obstacle and reenter the building. The bats may linger for several days trying to enter the structure. Once they determine that they cannot negotiate the drape, they seek shelter elsewhere. This revolutionary approach to structural pest management has proved successful in both residential and commercial structures.

Controlling garden pests means that you and not they can get the most enjoyment from your garden.

Glossary

Acute toxicant A chemical compound specifically formulated to kill rodents from a single feeding.

Aversive A chemical compound or physical device designed to change behavior from a negative experience.

Bait station A structure holding toxic baits constructed so that the animal must enter it to take the bait.

Browsing Feeding on leaves and shoots of woody plants.

Burrow A tunnel used for the storage of food, protective shelter, and the rearing of young.

Carnivore An animal that eats animal flesh.

Control To regulate or restrain the population of a pest species.

Crepuscular Activity occurring during dawn and dusk.

Depredation Damage of a crop by a pest species.

Estivation State of dormancy in an animal's activity cycle occurring during hot, dry summer months.

Exclusion Management option that prevents one or more animals or species from entering an area.

Food cache Food stored by an animal for future use.

Forb Any small broadleaf flowering plant.

Frightening device A device used to scare or drive away an animal pest. Examples include flags and noisemakers.

Fumigant Chemical substance that produces a toxic or suffocating gas.

Game animal An animal specified by state or federal game codes to be hunted for food or sport. Examples include deer, quail, ducks, and rabbits.

Gas cartridge Fumigant that produces a toxic or suffocating gas.

Girdling Gnawing damage caused by an animal encircling the trunk or limb of a woody plant.

Habitat Territory that supplies an animal or species with food, water, shelter, and space.

Habitat modification Altering the environment to make it less desirable to animal pests.

Herbivore An animal that eats only plants.

Hibernation State of dormancy in an animal's activity cycle occurring in winter.

Home range Territory used on a regular basis by an animal.

Insectivore An animal that eats insects.

Introduced species Species not native to an area that has been introduced through human intervention.

Lethal dose Defined quantity of a toxicant necessary to cause death.

Lethal methods or lethal techniques Management options that cause the death of the animal pest.

Live trap Trap designed to capture an animal without causing bodily harm.

Management Action that manipulates or impacts an animal's behavior through an understanding of the biological needs of the species.

Migrant bird Any species that makes an annual round trip between two geographic points or regions.

Native bird Bird that is an endemic species in an area.

Nongame animal Any animal not commonly hunted as specified in state or federal game codes. Examples include robins, warblers, mice, and native rats.

Nonlethal methods or nonlethal techniques Management options that do not cause the death of the animal pest.

Nontarget species Species that is not the object of any pest control action.

Omnivore An animal that eats both plant and animal foods.

Prebaiting Placing nontoxic bait to condition a targeted pest species to eat at a specific location before toxic baits are applied or to accustom a pest species to a trap.

Predator Any animal that survives by taking another animal (including insects) for food. Examples include moles, robins, and hawks.

Repellents Chemical or biological products designed to discourage an animal from damaging plants, trees, or structures.

Resident bird Bird species or individuals that live in an area the year around. An animal that does not migrate.

Ruminants Animals that have a multichambered stomach. Examples include deer, cattle, and sheep.

Runway A path that an animal commonly travels on or through.

Toxic bait Bait, usually formulated on a grain or cereal base, treated with a poison for the lethal control of an animal pest.

Trap crop A crop planted with the sole purpose of steering animal pests away from a preferred crop.

Untreated bait Bait that is not treated with a toxic substance. Used for prebaiting and on traps.

Wildlife pest Any species of wild animal that becomes a health hazard, causes economic damage, or is a general nuisance to people.

U.S. Measure and Metric Measure Conversion Chart

		Formulas for Exact Measures				Rounded Measures for Quick Reference		
	Symbol	When you know:	Multiply by:	To find:				
Mass (weight)	oz	ounces	28.35	grams		1 oz		= 30 g
	lb	pounds	0.45	kilograms		4 oz		= 115 g
	g	grams	0.035	ounces		8 oz		= 225 g
	kg	kilograms	2.2	pounds		16 oz	= 1 lb	= 450 g
						32 oz	= 2 lb	= 900 g
						36 oz	= 2¼ lb	= 1000 g (1 kg)
Volume	pt	pints	0.47	liters		1 c	= 8 oz	= 250 ml
	qt	quarts	0.95	liters		2 c (1 pt)	= 16 oz	= 500 ml
	gal	gallons	3.785	liters		4 c (1 qt)	= 32 oz	= 1 liter
	ml	milliliters	0.034	fluid ounces		4 qt (1 gal)	= 128 oz	= 3¾ liter
Length	in.	inches	2.54	centimeters		⅜ in.		= 1 cm
	ft	feet	30.48	centimeters		1 in.		= 2.5 cm
	yd	yards	0.9144	meters		2 in.		= 5 cm
	mi	miles	1.609	kilometers		2½ in.		= 6.5 cm
	km	kilometers	0.621	miles		12 in. (1 ft)		= 30 cm
	m	meters	1.094	yards		1 yd		= 90 cm
	cm	centimeters	0.39	inches		100 ft		= 30 m
						1 mi		= 1.6 km
Temperature	°F	Fahrenheit	⅝ (after subtracting 32)	Celsius		32°F		= 0°C
	°C	Celsius	⅞ (then add 32)	Fahrenheit		212°F		= 100°C
Area	in.²	square inches	6.452	square centimeters		1 in.²		= 6.5 cm²
	ft²	square feet	929.0	square centimeters		1 ft²		= 930 cm²
	yd²	square yards	8361.0	square centimeters		1 yd²		= 8360 cm²
	a.	acres	0.4047	hectares		1 a.		= 4050 m²